The Poetry of Ambrose Bierce - Volume 2

Ambrose Gwinnett Bierce had a diverse literary, military and journalistic career, during which his sardonic view of human nature ensured he was both frequently critical and frequently criticised. As a writer, his work included short stories, fables, editorials and his journalism, which was often controversial owing to his vehemence and acerbic style.

He was born on June 24th 1842 at Horse Cave Creek in Meigs Country, Ohio. His parents were poor and very religious but instilled in the young Bierce an abiding love of language and literature.

A year at the Kentucky Military Institute prepared him for the Civil War and a source of much of his acclaimed writing. Eventually he moved west to San Francisco where he married and began his literary career in earnest. A few years in England saw his work begin to publish in greater quantities

By 1891 although his marriage had fallen apart he had published 'An Occurrence at Owl Creek' his classic short story. To this he quickly added volumes of poetry and further volumes of stories and essays as well as a thriving career with the Hearst Organisation. In all his reputation was set as one of America's foremost literary creators.

At the age of 71, in 1913 Bierce departed from Washington, D.C., for a tour of the battlefields upon which he had fought during the civil war. He passed through Louisiana and Texas by December and was crossed into Mexico which was in the throes of revolution. He joined Pancho Villa's army as an observer. It was in Chihuahua where he wrote his last known communication dated 26th December 1913, closing with the words "as to me, I leave here tomorrow for an unknown destination" and then vanished without trace in what would become one of the most famous unexplained disappearances in American history.

Index of Contents
Emancipation
Exoneration
Expositor Veritatis
Fallen
Fame
Fame
Famine's Realm
Fate
Finis Aeternitatis
Fleet Strother
For A Certain Critic
For Mayor
For Merit
For President, Leland Stanford
For Tat
For Wounds
Foresight
Foundations Of The State
Four Candidates For Senator
Four Of A Kind

France
Francine
Freedom
From The Minutes
From Top To Bottom
From Virginia To Paris
General B.F. Butler
Genesis
George A. Knight
Geotheos
Haec Fabula Docet
Hell
History
Homo Podunkensis
Hospitality
Humility
Ignis Fatuus
In Contumaciam
In Defense
In High Life
In His Hand
In Memoriam
In The Binnacle
In Upper San Francisco
Incurable
Indicted
Industrial Discontent
Inspiration
Invocation
J.F.B.
James L. Flood
Johndonkey
Judex Judicatus
Judgment
Justice
L'audace
Laus Lucis
Liberty
Llewellen Powell
Lucifer Of The Torch
Lusus Politicus
Mad
Magnanimity
Master Of Three Arts
Matter For Gratitude
Mendax
Metempsychosis
Montague Leverson
Montefiore
Mr. Fink's Debating Donkey
Mr. Sheets

My Lord Poet
My Monument
Nanine
Nimrod
Not Guilty
Novum Organum
Omnes Vanitas
On A Proposed Crematory
On Stone
On The Platform
On The Wedding Of An Aeronaut
One And One Are Two
One Judge
One Mood's Expression
One Morning
One Of The Redeemed
One Of The Saints
One Of The Unfair Sex
One President
Oneiromancy
Ornithanthropos
Over The Border
Peace
'Phil' Crimmins
Philosopher Bimm
Piety
Poesy
Political Economy
Politics
Polyphemus
Posterity's Award
Prayer
Presentiment
Psychographs
Rebuke
Re-Edified
Rejected
Religion
Religious Progress
Reminded
Revenge
Rimer
Safety-Clutch
Salvini In America
Samuel Shortridge
Sires And Sons
Something In The Papers
Stephen Dorsey
Stephen J. Field
Stoneman In Heaven
Strained Relations

Substance Versus Shadow
Subterranean Phantasies
Surprised
T.A.H.
Technology
Tempora Mutantur
The Aesthetes
The American Party
The Barking Weasel
The Birth Of Virtue
The Boss's Choice
The Bride
The Committee On Public Morals
The Confederate Flags
The Convicts' Ball
The Cynic's Bequest
The Day Of Wrath / Dies Iræ
The Dead King
The Death Of Grant
The Debtor Abroad
The Division Superintendent
The Dying Statesman
The Eastern Question
The Fall Of Miss Larkin
The Following Pair
The Foot-Hill Resort
The Fountain Refilled
The Free Trader's Lament
The Fyghtynge Seventh
The Gates Ajar
The Genesis Of Embarrassment
The God's View-Point
The Hermit
The Hesitating Veteran
The Humorist
The In-Coming Climate
The Key Note
The King Of Bores
The Last Man
The Legatee
The Legend Of Immortal Truth
The Lord's Prayer On A Coin
The Lost Colonel
The Mackaiad
The Mad Philosopher
Ambrose Bierce - A Short Biography

Emancipation
Behold! the days of miracle at last

Return - if ever they were truly past:
From sinful creditors' unholy greed
The church called Calvary at last is freed
So called for there the Savior's crucified,
Roberts and Carmany on either side.
The circling contribution-box no more
Provokes the nod and simulated snore;
No more the Lottery, no more the Fair,
Lure the reluctant dollar from its lair,
Nor Ladies' Lunches at a bit a bite
Destroy the health yet spare the appetite,
While thrifty sisters o'er the cauldron stoop
To serve their God with zeal, their friends with soup,
And all the brethren mendicate the earth
With viewless placards: 'We've been so from birth!'
Sure of his wage, the pastor now can lend
His whole attention to his latter end,
Remarking with a martyr's prescient thrill
The Hemp maturing on the cheerless Hill.
The holy brethren, lifting pious palms,
Pour out their gratitude in prayer and psalms,
Chant De Profundis, meaning 'out of debt,'
And dance like mad - or would if they were let.
Deeply disguised (a deacon newly dead
Supplied the means) Jack Satan holds his head
As high as any and as loudly sings
His jubilate till each rafter rings.
'Rejoice, ye ever faithful,' bellows he,
'The debt is lifted and the temple free!'
Then says, aside, with gentle cachination:
'I've got a mortgage on the congregation.'

Exoneration

When men at candidacy don't connive,
From that suspicion if their friends would free 'em,
The teeth and nails with which they did not strive
Should be exhibited in a museum.

Expositor Veritatis

I Slept, and, waking in the years to be,
Heard voices, and approaching whence they came,
Listened indifferently where a key
Had lately been removed. An ancient dame
Said to her daughter: 'Go to yonder caddy
And get some emery to scour your daddy.'
And then I knew - some intuition said
That tombs were not and men had cleared their shelves

Of urns; and the electro-plated dead
Stood pedestaled as statues of themselves.
With famous dead men all the public places
Were thronged, and some in piles awaited bases.
One mighty structure's high facade alone
Contained a single monumental niche,
Where, central in that steep expanse of stone,
Gleamed the familiar form of Thomas Fitch.
A man cried: 'Lo! Truth's temple and its founder!'
Then gravely added: 'I'm her chief expounder.'

Fallen

O, hadst thou died when thou wert great,
When at thy feet a nation knelt
To sob the gratitude it felt
And thank the Saviour of the State,
Gods might have envied thee thy fate!
Then was the laurel round thy brow,
And friend and foe spoke praise of thee,
While all our hearts sang victory.
Alas! thou art too base to bow
To hide the shame that brands it now.

Fame

He held a book in his knotty paws,
And its title grand read he:
'The Chronicles of the Kings' it was,
By the History Companee.
'I'm a monarch,' he said
(But a tear he shed)
'And my picter here you see.
'Great and lasting is my renown,
However the wits may flout
As wide almost as this blessed town'
(But he winced as if with gout).
'I paid 'em like sin
For to put me in,
But it's O, and O, to be out!'

Fame

One thousand years I slept beneath the sod,
My sleep in 1901 beginning,
Then, by the action of some scurvy god
Who happened then to recollect my sinning,
I was revived and given another inning.

On breaking from my grave I saw a crowd
A formless multitude of men and women,
Gathered about a ruin. Clamors loud
I heard, and curses deep enough to swim in;
And, pointing at me, one said: 'Let's put him in.'
Then each turned on me with an evil look,
As in my ragged shroud I stood and shook.
'Nay, good Posterity,' I cried, 'forbear!
If that's a jail I fain would be remaining
Outside, for truly I should little care
To catch my death of cold. I'm just regaining
The life lost long ago by my disdaining
To take precautions against draughts like those
That, haply, penetrate that cracked and splitting
Old structure.' Then an aged wight arose
From a chair of state in which he had been sitting,
And with preliminary coughing, spitting
And wheezing, said: "T is not a jail, we're sure,
Whate'er it may have been when it was newer.
"T was found two centuries ago, o'ergrown
With brush and ivy, all undoored, ungated;
And in restoring it we found a stone
Set here and there in the dilapidated
And crumbling frieze, inscribed, in antiquated
Big characters, with certain uncouth names,
Which we conclude were borne of old by awful
Rapscallions guilty of all sinful games
Vagrants engaged in purposes unlawful,
And orators less sensible than jawful.
So each ten years we add to the long row
A name, the most unworthy that we know.'
'But why,' I asked, 'put me in?' He replied:
'You look it' and the judgment pained me greatly;
Right gladly would I then and there have died,
But that I'd risen from the grave so lately.
But on examining that solemn, stately
Old ruin I remarked: 'My friend, you err
The truth of this is just what I expected.
This building in its time made quite a stir.
I lived (was famous, too) when 't was erected.
The names here first inscribed were much respected.
This is the Hall of Fame, or I'm a stork,
And this goat pasture once was called New York.'

Famine's Realm
To him in whom the love of Nature has
Imperfectly supplanted the desire
And dread necessity of food, your shore,
Fair Oakland, is a terror. Over all

Your sunny level, from Tamaletown
To where the Pestuary's fragrant slime,
With dead dogs studded, bears its ailing fleet,
Broods the still menace of starvation. Bones
Of men and women bleach along the ways
And pampered vultures sleep upon the trees.
It is a land of death, and Famine there
Holds sovereignty; though some there be her sway
Who challenge, and intrenched in larders live,
Drawing their sustentation from abroad.
But woe to him, the stranger! He shall die
As die the early righteous in the bud
And promise of their prime. He, venturesome
To penetrate the wilds rectangular
Of grass-grown ways luxuriant of blooms,
Frequented of the bee and of the blithe,
Bold squirrel, strays with heedless feet afar
From human habitation and is lost
In mid-Broadway. There hunger seizes him,
And (careless man! deeming God's providence
Extends so far) he has not wherewithal
To bate its urgency. Then, lo! appears
A mealery - a restaurant - a place
Where poison battles famine, and the two,
Like fish-hawks warring in the upper sky
For that which one has taken from the deep,
Manage between them to dispatch the prey.
He enters and leaves hope behind. There ends
His history. Anon his bones, clean-picked
By buzzards (with the bones himself had picked,
Incautious) line the highway. O, my friends,
Of all felonious and deadlywise
Devices of the Enemy of Souls,
Planted along the ways of life to snare
Man's mortal and immortal part alike,
The Oakland restaurant is chief. It lives
That man may die. It flourishes that life
May wither. Its foundation stones repose
On human hearts and hopes. I've seen in it
Crabs stewed in milk and salad offered up
With dressing so unholily compound
That it included flour and sugar! Yea,
I've eaten dog there! dog, as I'm a man,
Dog seethed in sewage of the town! No more
Thy hand, Dyspepsia, assumes the pen
And scrawls a tortured 'Finis' on the page.

Fate
Alas, alas, for the tourist's guide!

He turned from the beaten trail aside,
Wandered bewildered, lay down and died.
O grim is the Irony of Fate:
It switches the man of low estate
And loosens the dogs upon the great.
It lights the fireman to roast the cook;
The fisherman squirms upon the hook,
And the flirt is slain with a tender look.
The undertaker it overtakes;
It saddles the cavalier, and makes
The haughtiest butcher into steaks.
Assist me, gods, to balk the decree!
Nothing I'll do and nothing I'll be,
In order that nothing be done to me.

Finis Aeternitatis
Strolling at sunset in my native land,
With fruits and flowers thick on either hand,
I crossed a Shadow flung athwart my way,
Emerging on a waste of rock and sand.
'The apples all are gone from here,' I said,
'The roses perished and their spirits fled.
I will go back.' A voice cried out: 'The man
Is risen who eternally was dead!'
I turned and saw an angel standing there,
Newly descended from the heights of air.
Sweet-eyed compassion filled his face, his hands
A naked sword and golden trumpet bare.
'Nay, 'twas not death, the shadow that I crossed,'
I said. 'Its chill was but a touch of frost.
It made me gasp, but quickly I came through,
With breath recovered ere it scarce was lost.'
'Twas the same land! Remembered mountains thrust
Grayed heads asky, and every dragging gust,
In ashen valleys where my sons had reaped,
Stirred in familiar river-beds the dust.
Some heights, where once the traveler was shown
The youngest and the proudest city known,
Lifted smooth ridges in the steely light
Bleak, desolate acclivities of stone.
Where I had worshiped at my father's tomb,
Within a massive temple's awful gloom,
A jackal slunk along the naked rock,
Affrighted by some prescience of doom.
Man's vestiges were nowhere to be found,
Save one brass mausoleum on a mound
(I knew it well) spared by the artist Time
To emphasize the desolation round.
Into the stagnant sea the sullen sun

Sank behind bars of crimson, one by one.
'Eternity's at hand!' I cried aloud.
'Eternity,' the angel said, 'is done.
For man is ages dead in every zone;
The angels all are dead but I alone;
The devils, too, are cold enough at last,
And God lies dead before the great white throne!
'Tis foreordained that I bestride the shore
When all are gone (as Gabriel did before,

When I had throttled the last man alive)
And swear Eternity shall be no more.'
'O Azrael O Prince of Death, declare
Why conquered I the grave?' I cried. 'What rare,
Conspicuous virtues won this boon for me?'
'You've been revived,' he said, 'to hear me swear.'
'Then let me creep again beneath the grass,
And knock thou at yon pompous tomb of brass.
If ears are what you want, Charles Crocker's there
Betwixt the greatest ears, the greatest ass.'
He rapped, and while the hollow echoes rang,
Out at the door a curst hyena sprang
And fled! Said Azrael: 'His soul's escaped,'
And closed the brazen portal with a bang.

Fleet Strother

What! you were born, you animated doll,
Within the shadow of the Capitol?
'Twas always thought (and Bancroft so assures
His trusting readers) it was reared in yours.

For A Certain Critic

Let lowly themes engage my humble pen
Stupidities of critics, not of men.
Be it mine once more the maunderings to trace
Of the expounders' self-directed race
Their wire-drawn fancies, finically fine,
Of diligent vacuity the sign.
Let them in jargon of their trade rehearse
The moral meaning of the random verse
That runs spontaneous from the poet's pen
To be half-blotted by ambitious men
Who hope with his their meaner names to link
By writing o'er it in another ink
The thoughts unreal which they think they think,
Until the mental eye in vain inspects
The hateful palimpsest to find the text.

The lark ascending heavenward, loud and long
Sings to the dawning day his wanton song.
The moaning dove, attentive to the sound,
Its hidden meaning hastens to expound:
Explains its principles, design-in brief,
Pronounces it a parable of grief!
The bee, just pausing ere he daubs his thigh
With pollen from a hollyhock near by,
Declares he never heard in terms so just
The labor problem thoughtfully discussed!
The browsing ass looks up and clears his whistle
To say: 'A monologue upon the thistle!'
Meanwhile the lark, descending, folds his wing
And innocently asks: 'What! did I sing?'
O literary parasites! who thrive
Upon the fame of better men, derive
Your sustenance by suction, like a leech,
And, for you preach of them, think masters preach,
Who find it half is profit, half delight,
To write about what you could never write,
Consider, pray, how sharp had been the throes
Of famine and discomfiture in those
You write of if they had been critics, too,
And doomed to write of nothing but of you!
Lo! where the gaping crowd throngs yonder tent,
To see the lion resolutely bent!
The prosing showman who the beast displays
Grows rich and richer daily in its praise.
But how if, to attract the curious yeoman,
The lion owned the show and showed the showman?

For Mayor
O Abner Doble - whose 'catarrhal name'
Budd of that ilk might envy - 'tis a rough
Rude thing to say, but it is plain enough
Your name is to be sneezed at: its acclaim
Will 'fill the speaking trump of future fame'
With an impeded utterance - a puff
Suggesting that a pinch or two of snuff
Would clear the tube and somewhat disinflame.
Nay, Abner Doble, you'll not get from me
My voice and influence: I'll cheer instead,
Some other man; for when my voice ascends a
Tall pinnacle of praise, and at high C
Sustains a chosen name, it shan't be said
My influence is naught but influenza.

For Merit
To Parmentier Parisians raise
A statue fine and large:
He cooked potatoes fifty ways,
Nor ever led a charge.
'Palmam qui meruit' - the rest
You knew as well as I;
And best of all to him that best
Of sayings will apply.
Let meaner men the poet's bays
Or warrior's medal wear;
Who cooks potatoes fifty ways
Shall bear the palm-de terre.

For President, Leland Stanford
Mahomet Stanford, with covetous stare,
Gazed on a vision surpassingly fair:
Far on the desert's remote extreme
A mountain of gold with a mellow gleam
Reared its high pinnacles into the sky,
The work of mirage to delude the eye.
Pixley Pasha, at the Prophet's feet
Piously licking them, swearing them sweet,
Ventured, observing his master's glance,
To beg that he order the mountain's advance.
Mahomet Stanford exerted his will,
Commanding: 'In Allah's name, hither, hill!'
Never an inch the mountain came.
Mahomet Stanford, with face aflame,
Lifted his foot and kicked, alack!
Pixley Pasha on the end of the back.
Mollified thus and smiling free,
He said: 'Since the mountain won't come to me,
I'll go to the mountain.' With infinite pains,
Camels in caravans, negroes in trains,
Warriors, workmen, women, and fools,
Food and water and mining tools
He gathered about him, a mighty array,
And the journey began at the close of day.
All night they traveled, at early dawn
Many a wearisome league had gone.
Morning broke fair with a golden sheen,
Mountain, alas, was nowhere seen!
Mahomet Stanford pounded his breast,
Pixley Pasha he thus addressed:
'Dog of mendacity, cheat and slave,
May jackasses sing o'er your grandfather's grave!'

For Tat

O, heavenly powers! will wonders never cease?
Hair upon dogs and feathers upon geese!
The boys in mischief and the pigs in mire!
The drinking water wet! the coal on fire!
In meadows, rivulets surpassing fair,
Forever running, yet forever there!
A tail appended to the gray baboon!
A person coming out of a saloon!
Last, and of all most marvelous to see,
A female Yahoo flinging filth at me!
If 'twould but stick I'd bear upon my coat
May Little's proof that she is fit to vote.

For Wounds

O bear me, gods, to some enchanted isle
Where woman's tears can antidote her smile.

Foresight

An 'actors' cemetery'! Sure
The devil never tires
Of planning places to procure
The sticks to feed his fires.

Foundations Of The State

Observe, dear Lord, what lively pranks
Are played by sentimental cranks!
First this one mounts his hinder hoofs
And brays the chimneys off the roofs;
Then that one, with exalted voice,
Expounds the thesis of his choice,
Our understandings to bombard,
Till all the window panes are starred!
A third augments the vocal shock
Till steeples to their bases rock,
Confessing, as they humbly nod,
They hear and mark the will of God.
A fourth in oral thunder vents
His awful penury of sense
Till dogs with sympathetic howls,
And lowing cows, and cackling fowls,
Hens, geese, and all domestic birds,
Attest the wisdom of his words.
Cranks thus their intellects deflate

Of theories about the State.
This one avers 'tis built on Truth,
And that on Temperance. This youth
Declares that Science bears the pile;
That graybeard, with a holy smile,
Says Faith is the supporting stone;
While women swear that Love alone
Could so unflinchingly endure
The heavy load. And some are sure
The solemn vow of Christian Wedlock
Is the indubitable bedrock.
Physicians once about the bed
Of one whose life was nearly sped
Blew up a disputatious breeze
About the cause of his disease:
This, that and t' other thing they blamed.
'Tut, tut!' the dying man exclaimed,
'What made me ill I do not care;
You've not an ounce of it, I'll swear.
And if you had the skill to make it
I'd see you hanged before I'd take it!'

Four Candidates For Senator

To flatter your way to the goad of your hope,
O plausible Mr. Perkins,
You'll need ten tons of the softest soap
And butter a thousand firkins.
The soap you could put to a better use
In washing your hands of ambition
Ere the butter's used for cooking your goose
To a beautiful brown condition.
'The Railroad can't run Stanford.' That is so
The tail can't curl the pig; but then, you know,
Inside the vegetable-garden's pale
The pig will eat more cabbage than the tail.
When Sargent struts by all the lawmakers say:
'Right - left!' It is fair to infer
The right will get left, nor polar the day
When he makes that thing to occur.
Not so, not so, 'tis a joke, that cry
Foolish and dull and small:
He so bores them for votes that they mean to imply
He's a drill-Sargent, that is all.
Gods! what a sight! Astride McClure's broad back
Estee jogs round the Senatorial track,
The crowd all undecided, as they pass,
Whether to cheer the man or cheer the ass.
They stop: the man to lower his feet is seen
And the tired beast, withdrawing from between,

Mounts, as they start again, the biped's neck,
And scarce the crowd can say which one's on deck.

Four Of A Kind
ROBERT F. MORROW
Dear man! although a stranger and a foe
To soft affection's humanizing glow;
Although untaught how manly hearts may throb
With more desires than the desire to rob;
Although as void of tenderness as wit,
And owning nothing soft but Maurice Schmitt;
Although polluted, shunned and in disgrace,
You fill me with a passion to embrace!
Attentive to your look, your smile, your beck,
I watch and wait to fall upon your neck.
Lord of my love, and idol of my hope,
You are my Valentine, and I'm
A ROPE.

ALFRED CLARKE JR.
Illustrious son of an illustrious sire
Entrusted with the duty to cry 'Fire!'
And call the engines out, exert your power
With care. When, looking from your lofty tower,
You see a ruddy light on every wall,
Pause for a moment ere you sound the call:
It may be from a fire, it may be, too,
From good men's blushes when they think of you.

JUDGE RUTLEDGE
Sultan of Stupids! with enough of brains
To go indoors in all uncommon rains,
But not enough to stay there when the storm
Is past. When all the world is dry and warm,
In irking comfort, lamentably gay,
Keeping the evil tenor of your way,
You walk abroad, sweet, beautiful and smug,
And Justice hears you with her wonted shrug,
Lifts her broad bandage half-an-inch and keeps
One eye upon you while the other weeps.

W.H.L. BARNES
Happy the man who sin's proverbial wage
Receives on the instalment plan-in age.
For him the bulldog pistol's honest bark
Has naught of terror in its blunt remark.
He looks with calmness on the gleaming steel
If e'er it touched his heart he did not feel:
Superior hardness turned its point away,
Though urged by fond affinity to stay;
His bloodless veins ignored the futile stroke,
And moral mildew kept the cut in cloak.

Happy the man, I say, to whom the wage
Of sin has been commuted into age.
Yet not quite happy-hark, that horrid cry!
His cruel mirror wounds him in the eye!

France

Unhappy State! with horrors still to strive:
Thy Hugo dead, thy Boulanger alive;
A Prince who'd govern where he dares not dwell,
And who for power would his birthright sell
Who, anxious o'er his enemies to reign,
Grabs at the scepter and conceals the chain;
While pugnant factions mutually strive
By cutting throats to keep the land alive.
Perverse in passion, as in pride perverse
To all a mistress, to thyself a curse;
Sweetheart of Europe! every sun's embrace
Matures the charm and poison of thy grace.
Yet time to thee nor peace nor wisdom brings:
In blood of citizens and blood of kings
The stones of thy stability are set,
And the fair fabric trembles at a threat.

Francine

Did I believe the angels soon would call
You, my beloved, to the other shore,
And I should never see you any more,
I love you so I know that I should fall
Into dejection utterly, and all
Love's pretty pageantry, wherein we bore
Twin banners bravely in the tumult's fore,
Would seem as shadows idling on a wall.
So daintily I love you that my love
Endures no rumor of the winter's breath,
And only blossoms for it thinks the sky
Forever gracious, and the stars above
Forever friendly. Even the fear of death
Were frost wherein its roses all would die.

Freedom

Freedom, as every schoolboy knows,
Once shrieked as Kosciusko fell;
On every wind, indeed, that blows
I hear her yell.
She screams whenever monarchs meet,

And parliaments as well,
To bind the chains about her feet
And toll her knell.
And when the sovereign people cast
The votes they cannot spell,
Upon the pestilential blast
Her clamors swell.
For all to whom the power's given
To sway or to compel,
Among themselves apportion Heaven
And give her Hell.
Blary O'Gary.

From The Minutes

When, with the force of a ram that discharges its ponderous body
Straight at the rear elevation of the luckless culler of simples,
The foot of Herculean Kilgore-statesman of surname suggestive
Or carnage unspeakable! lit like a missile prodigious
Upon the Congressional door with a monstrous and mighty momentum,
Causing that vain ineffective bar to political freedom
To fly from its hinges, effacing the nasal excrescence of Dingley,
That luckless one, decently veiling the ruin with ready bandanna,
Lamented the loss of his eminence, sadly with sobs as follows:
'Ah, why was I ever elected to the halls of legislation,
So soon to be shown the door with pitiless emphasis?
Truly, I've leaned on a broken Reed, and the same has gone back on me meanly.
Where now is my prominence, erstwhile in council conspicuous, patent?
Alas, I did never before understand what I now see clearly,
To wit, that Democracy tends to level all human distinctions!'
His fate so untoward and sad the Pine-tree statesman, bewailing,
Stood in the corridor there while Democrats freed from confinement
Came trooping forth from the chamber, dissembling all, as they passed him,
Hilarious sentiments painful indeed to observe, and remarking:
'O friend and colleague of the Speaker, what ails the unjoyous proboscis?'

From Top To Bottom

O Buddha, had you but foreknown
The vices of your priesthood
It would have made you twist and moan
As any wounded beast would.
You would have damned the entire lot
And turned a Christian, would you not?
There were no Christians, I'll allow,
In your day; that would only
Have brought distinction. Even now
A Christian might feel lonely.
All take the name, but facts are things

As stubborn as the will of kings.
The priests were ignorant and low
When ridiculed by Lucian;
The records, could we read, might show
The same of times Confucian.
And yet the fact I can't disguise
That Deacon Rankin's good and wise.
'Tis true he is not quite a priest,
Nor more than half a preacher;
But he exhorts as loud at least
As any living creature.
And when the plate is passed about
He never takes a penny out.
From Buddha down to Rankin! There,
I never did intend to.
This pen's a buzzard's quill, I swear,
Such subjects to descend to.
When from the humming-bird I've wrung
A plume I'll write of Mike de Young.

From Virginia To Paris
The polecat, sovereign of its native wood,
Dashes damnation upon bad and good;
The health of all the upas trees impairs
By exhalations deadlier than theirs;
Poisons the rattlesnake and warts the toad
The creeks go rotten and the rocks corrode!
She shakes o'er breathless hill and shrinking dale
The horrid aspergillus of her tail!
From every saturated hair, till dry,
The spargent fragrances divergent fly,
Deafen the earth and scream along the sky!
Removed to alien scenes, amid the strife
Of urban odors to ungladden life
Where gas and sewers and dead dogs conspire
The flesh to torture and the soul to fire
Where all the 'well defined and several stinks'
Known to mankind hold revel and high jinks
Humbled in spirit, smitten with a sense
Of lost distinction, leveled eminence,
She suddenly resigns her baleful trust,
Nor ever lays again our mortal dust.
Her powers atrophied, her vigor sunk,
She lives deodorized, a sweeter skunk.

General B.F. Butler
Thy flesh to earth, thy soul to God,

We gave, O gallant brother;
And o'er thy grave the awkward squad
Fired into one another!

Genesis

God said, 'Let there be Crime,' and the command
Brought Satan, leading Stoneman by the hand.
'Why, that's Stupidity, not Crime,' said God
'Bring what I ordered.' Satan with a nod
Replied, 'This is one element - when I
The other - Opportunity - supply
In just equivalent, the two'll affine
And in a chemical embrace combine
And Crime result - for Crime can only be
Stupiditate of Opportunity.'
So leaving Stoneman (not as yet endowed
With soul) in special session on a cloud,
Nick to his sooty laboratory went,
Returning soon with t'other element.
'Here's Opportunity,' he said, and put
Pen, ink, and paper down at Stoneman's foot.
He seized them - Heaven was filled with fires and thunders,
And Crime was added to Creation's wonders!

George A. Knight

Attorney Knight, it happens so sometimes
That lawyers, justifying cut-throats' crimes
For hire - calumniating, too, for gold,
The dead, dumb victims cruelly unsouled
Speak, through the press, to a tribunal far
More honorable than their Honors are,
A court that sits not with assenting smile
While living rogues dead gentleman revile,
A court where scoundrel ethics of your trade
Confuse no judgment and no cheating aid,
The Court of Honest Souls, where you in vain
May plead your right to falsify for gain,
Sternly reminded if a man engage
To serve assassins for the liar's wage,
His mouth with vilifying falsehoods crammed,
He's twice detestable and doubly damned!
Attorney Knight, defending Powell, you,
To earn your fee, so energetic grew
(So like a hound, the pride of all the pack,
Clapping your nose upon the dead man's track
To run his faults to earth - at least proclaim
At vacant holes the overtaken game)

That men who marked you nourishing the tongue,
And saw your arms so vigorously swung,
All marveled how so light a breeze could stir
So great a windmill to so great a whirr!
Little they knew, or surely they had grinned,
The mill was laboring to raise the wind.
Ralph Smith a 'shoulder-striker'! God, O hear
This hardy man's description of thy dear
Dead child, the gentlest soul, save only One,
E'er born in any land beneath the sun.
All silent benefactions still he wrought:
High deed and gracious speech and noble thought,
Kept all thy law, and, seeking still the right,
Upon his blameless breast received the light.
'Avenge, O Lord, thy slaughtered saints,' he cried
Whose wrath was deep as his comparison wide
Milton, thy servant. Nay, thy will be done:
To smite or spare, to me it all is one.
Can vengeance bring my sorrow to an end,
Or justice give me back my buried friend?
But if some Milton vainly now implore,
And Powell prosper as he did before,
Yet 'twere too much that, making no ado,
Thy saints be slaughtered and be slandered too.
So, Lord, make Knight his weapon keep in sheath,
Or do Thou wrest it from between his teeth!

Geotheos

As sweet as the look of a lover
Saluting the eyes of a maid
That blossom to blue as the maid
Is ablush to the glances above her,
The sunshine is gilding the glade
And lifting the lark out of shade.
Sing therefore high praises, and therefore
Sing songs that are ancient as gold,
Of earth in her garments of gold;
Nor ask of their meaning, nor wherefore
They charm as of yore, for behold!
The Earth is as fair as of old.
Sing songs of the pride of the mountains,
And songs of the strength of the seas,
And the fountains that fall to the seas
From the hands of the hills, and the fountains
That shine in the temples of trees,
In valleys of roses and bees.
Sing songs that are dreamy and tender,
Of slender Arabian palms,
And shadows that circle the palms,

Where caravans out of the splendor,
Are kneeling in blossoms and balms,
In islands of infinite calms.
Barbaric, O Man, was thy runing
When mountains were stained as with wine
By the dawning of Time, and as wine
Were the seas, yet its echoes are crooning,
Achant in the gusty pine
And the pulse of the poet's line.

Haec Fabula Docet

A rat who'd gorged a box of bane
And suffered an internal pain,
Came from his hole to die (the label
Required it if the rat were able)
And found outside his habitat
A limpid stream. Of bane and rat
'T was all unconscious; in the sun
It ran and prattled just for fun.
Keen to allay his inward throes,
The beast immersed his filthy nose
And drank, then, bloated by the stream,
And filled with superheated steam,
Exploded with a rascal smell,
Remarking, as his fragments fell
Astonished in the brook: 'I'm thinking
This water's damned unwholesome drinking!'

Hell

The friends who stood about my bed
Looked down upon my face and said:
'God's will be done, the fellow's dead.'
When from my body I was free
I straightway felt myself, ah me!
Sink downward to the life to be.
Full twenty centuries I fell,
And then alighted. 'Here you dwell
For aye,' a Voice cried 'this is Hell!'
A landscape lay about my feet,
Where trees were green and flowers sweet.
The climate was devoid of heat.
The sun looked down with gentle beam
Upon the bosom of the stream,
Nor saw I any sign of steam.
The waters by the sky were tinged,
The hills with light and color fringed.
Birds warbled on the wing unsinged.

'Ah, no, this is not Hell,' I cried;
'The preachers ne'er so greatly lied.
This is Earth's spirit glorified!
'Good souls do not in Hades dwell,
And, look, there's John P. Irish!' 'Well,'
The Voice said, 'that's what makes it Hell.'

History

What wrecked the Roman power? One says vice,
Another indolence, another dice.
Emascle says polygamy. 'Not so,'
Says Impycu ''twas luxury and show.'
The parson, lifting up a brow of brass,
Swears superstition gave the coup de grace,
Great Allison, the statesman-chap affirms
'Twas lack of coins (croaks Medico: ''T was worms')
And John P. Jones the swift suggestion collars,
Averring the no coins were silver dollars.
Thus, through the ages, each presuming quack
Turns the poor corpse upon its rotten back,
Holds a new 'autopsy' and finds that death
Resulted partly from the want of breath,
But chiefly from some visitation sad
That points his argument or serves his fad.
They're all in error - never human mind
The cause of the disaster has divined.
What slew the Roman power? Well, provided
You'll keep the secret, I will tell you. I did.

Homo Podunkensis

As the poor ass that from his paddock strays
Might sound abroad his field-companions' praise,
Recounting volubly their well-bred leer,
Their port impressive and their wealth of ear,
Mistaking for the world's assent the clang
Of echoes mocking his accurst harangue;
So the dull clown, untraveled though at large,
Visits the city on the ocean's marge,
Expands his eyes and marvels to remark
Each coastwise schooner and each alien bark;
Prates of 'all nations,' wonders as he stares
That native merchants sell imported wares,
Nor comprehends how in his very view
A foreign vessel has a foreign crew;
Yet, faithful to the hamlet of his birth,
Swears it superior to aught on earth,
Sighs for the temples locally renowned

The village school-house and the village pound
And chalks upon the palaces of Rome
The peasant sentiments of 'Home, Sweet Home!'

Hospitality
Why ask me, Gastrogogue, to dine
(Unless to praise your rascal wine)
Yet never ask some luckless sinner
Who needs, as I do not, a dinner?

Humility
Great poets fire the world with fagots big
That make a crackling racket,
But I'm content with but a whispering twig
To warm some single jacket.

Ignis Fatuus
Weep, weep, each loyal partisan,
For Buckley, king of hearts;
A most accomplished man; a man
Of parts - of foreign parts.
Long years he ruled with gentle sway,
Nor grew his glory dim;
And he would be with us to-day
If we were but with him.
Men wondered at his going off
In such a sudden way;
'Twas thought, as he had come to scoff
He would remain to prey.
Since he is gone we're all agreed
That he is what men call
A crook: his very steps, indeed,
Are bent to Montreal.
So let our tears unhindered flow,
Our sighs and groans have way:
It matters not how much we Oh!
The devil is to pay.

In Contumaciam
Och! Father McGlynn,
Ye appear to be in
Fer a bit of a bout wid the Pope;
An' there's divil a doubt

But he's knockin' ye out
While ye're hangin' onto the rope.
An' soon ye'll lave home
To thravel to Rome,
For its bound to Canossa ye are.
Persistin' to shtay
When ye're ordered away
Bedad! that is goin' too far!

In Defense

You may say, if you please, Johnny Bull, that our girls
Are crazy to marry your dukes and your earls;
But I've heard that the maids of your own little isle
Greet bachelor lords with a favoring smile.
Nay, titles, 'tis said in defense of our fair,
Are popular here because popular there;
And for them our ladies persistently go
Because 'tis exceedingly English, you know.
Whatever the motive, you'll have to confess
The effort's attended with easy success;
And - pardon the freedom - 'tis thought, over here,
'Tis mortification you mask with a sneer.
It's all very well, sir, your scorn to parade
Of the high nasal twang of the Yankee maid,
But, ah, to my lord when he dares to propose
No sound is so sweet as that 'Yes' from the nose.
Our ladies, we grant, walk alone in the street
(Observe, by-the-by, on what delicate feet!)
'Tis a habit they got here at home, where they say
The men from politeness go seldom astray.
Ah, well, if the dukes and the earls and that lot
Can stand it (God succor them if they cannot!)
Your commoners ought to assent, I am sure,
And what they're not called on to suffer, endure.
"'Tis nothing but money?' 'Your nobles are bought?'
As to that, I submit, it is commonly thought
That England's a country not specially free
Of Croesi and (if you'll allow it) Croesae.
You've many a widow and many a girl
With money to purchase a duke or an earl.
'Tis a very remarkable thing, you'll agree,
When goods import buyers from over the sea.
Alas for the woman of Albion's isle!
She may simper; as well as she can she may smile;
She may wear pantalettes and an air of repose
But my lord of the future will talk through his nose.

In High Life

Sir Impycu Lackland, from over the sea,
Has led to the altar Miss Bloatie Bondee.
The wedding took place at the Church of St. Blare;
The fashion, the rank and the wealth were all there
No person was absent of all whom one meets.
Lord Mammon himself bowed them into their seats,
While good Sir John Satan attended the door
And Sexton Beelzebub managed the floor,
Respectfully keeping each dog to its rug,
Preserving the peace between poodle and pug.
Twelve bridesmaids escorted the bride up the aisle
To blush in her blush and to smile in her smile;
Twelve groomsmen supported the eminent groom
To scowl in his scowl and to gloom in his gloom.
The rites were performed by the hand and the lip
Of his Grace the Diocesan, Billingham Pip,
Assisted by three able-bodied divines.
He prayed and they grunted, he read, they made signs.
Such fashion, such beauty, such dressing, such grace
Were ne'er before seen in that heavenly place!
That night, full of gin, and all blazing inside,
Sir Impycu blackened the eyes of his bride.

In His Hand

De Young (in Chicago the story is told)
'Took his life in his hand,' like a warrior bold,
And stood before Buckley - who thought him behind,
For Buckley, the man-eating monster is blind.
'Count fairly the ballots!' so rang the demand
Of the gallant De Young, with his life in his hand.
'Tis done, and the struggle is ended. No more
He havocs the battle-field, gilt with the gore
Of slain reputations. No more he defies
His 'lying opponents' with deadlier lies.
His trumpet is hushed and his belt is unbound
His enemies' characters cumber the ground.
They bloat on the war-plain with ink all asoak,
The fortunate candidates perching to croak.
No more he will charge, with a daring divine,
His foes with corruption, his friends by the line.
The thunders are stilled of the horrid campaign,
De Young is triumphant, and never again
Will he need, with his life in his hand, to roar:
'Count fair or, by G--, I will die on your floor!'
His life has been spared, for his sins to atone,
And the hand that he took it in washed with cologne.

In Memoriam

Beauty (they called her) wasn't a maid
Of many things in the world afraid.
She wasn't a maid who turned and fled
At sight of a mouse, alive or dead.
She wasn't a maid a man could 'shoo'
By shouting, however abruptly, 'Boo!'
She wasn't a maid who'd run and hide
If her face and figure you idly eyed.
She was'nt a maid who'd blush and shake
When asked what part of the fowl she'd take.
(I blush myself to confess she preferred,
And commonly got, the most of the bird.)
She wasn't a maid to simper because
She was asked to sing, if she ever was.
In short, if the truth must be displayed
In puris - Beauty wasn't a maid.
Beauty, furry and fine and fat,
Yawny and clawy, sleek and all that,
Was a pampered and spoiled Angora cat!
I loved her well, and I'm proud that she
Wasn't indifferent, quite, to me;
In fact I have sometimes gone so far
(You know, mesdames, how silly men are)
As to think she preferred - excuse the conceit
My legs upon which to sharpen her feet.
Perhaps it shouldn't have gone for much,
But I started and thrilled beneath her touch!
Ah, well, that's ancient history now:
The fingers of Time have touched my brow,
And I hear with never a start to-day
That Beauty has passed from the earth away.
Gone! her death-song (it killed her) sung.
Gone! her fiddlestrings all unstrung.
Gone to the bliss of a new regime
Of turkey smothered in seas of cream;
Of roasted mice (a superior breed,
To science unknown and the coarser need
Of the living cat) cooked by the flame
Of the dainty soul of an erring dame
Who gave to purity all her care,
Neglecting the duty of daily prayer,
Crisp, delicate mice, just touched with spice
By the ghost of a breeze from Paradise;
A very digestible sort of mice.
Let scoffers sneer, I propose to hold
That Beauty has mounted the Stair of Gold,
To eat and eat, forever and aye,
On a velvet rug from a golden tray.

But the human spirit - that is my creed
Rots in the ground like a barren seed.
That is my creed, abhorred by Man
But approved by Cat since time began.
Till Death shall kick at me, thundering 'Scat!'
I shall hold to that, I shall hold to that.

In The Binnacle

The Church's compass, if you please,
Has two or three (or more) degrees
Of variation;
And many a soul has gone to grief
On this or that or t'other reef
Through faith unreckoning or brief
Miscalculation.
Misguidance is of perils chief
To navigation.
The obsequious thing makes, too, you'll mark,
Obeisance through a little arc
Of declination;
For Satan, fearing witches, drew
From Death's pale horse, one day, a shoe,
And nailed it to his door to undo
Their machination.
Since then the needle dips to woo
His habitation.

In Upper San Francisco

I heard that Heaven was bright and fair,
And politicians dwelt not there.
'Twas said by knowing ones that they
Were in the Elsewhere - so to say.
So, waking from my last long sleep,
I took my place among the sheep.
I passed the gate - Saint Peter eyed
Me sharply as I stepped inside.
He thought, as afterward I learned,
That I was Chris, the Unreturned.
The new Jerusalem - ah me,
It was a sorry sight to see!
The mansions of the blest were there,
And mostly they were fine and fair;
But O, such streets! so deep and wide,
And all unpaved, from side to side!
And in a public square there grew
A blighted tree, most sad to view.
From off its trunk the bark was ripped

Its very branches all were stripped!
An angel perched upon the fence
With all the grace of indolence.
'Celestial bird,' I cried, in pain,
'What vandal wrought this wreck? Explain.'
He raised his eyelids as if tired:
'What is a Vandal?' he inquired.
'This is the Tree of Life. 'Twas stripped
By Durst and Siebe, who have shipped
'The bark across the Jordan - see?
And sold it to a tannery.'
'Alas,' I sighed, 'their old-time tricks!
That pavement, too, of golden bricks
'They've gobbled that?' But with a scowl,
'You greatly wrong them,' said the fowl:
''Twas Gilleran did that, I fear

Head of the Street Department here.'
'What! what!' cried I - 'you let such chaps
Come here? You've Satan, too, perhaps.'
'We had him, yes, but off he went,
Yet showed some purpose to repent;
'But since your priests and parsons filled
The place with those their preaching killed'
(Here Siebe passed along with Durst,
Psalming as if their lungs would burst)
'He swears his foot no more shall press
('Tis cloven, anyhow, I guess)
'Our soil. In short, he's out on strike
But devils are not all alike.'
Lo! Gilleran came down the street,
Pressing the soil with broad, flat feet!

Incurable

From pride, joy, hate, greed, melancholy
From any kind of vice, or folly,
Bias, propensity or passion
That is in prevalence and fashion,
Save one, the sufferer or lover
May, by the grace of God, recover:
Alone that spiritual tetter,
The zeal to make creation better,
Glows still immedicably warmer.
Who knows of a reformed reformer?

Indicted

Dear Bruner, once we had a little talk

(That is to say, 'twas I did all the talking)
About the manner of your moral walk:
How devious the trail you made in stalking,
On level ground, your law-protected game
'Another's Dollar' is, I think, its name.
Your crooked course more recently is not
So blamable; for, truly, you have stumbled
On evil days; and 'tis your luckless lot
To traverse spaces (with a spirit humbled,
Contrite, dejected and divinely sad)
Where, 'tis confessed, the walking's rather bad.
Jordan, the song says, is a road (I thought
It was a river) that is hard to travel;
And Dublin, if you'd find it, must be sought
Along a highway with more rocks than gravel.
In difficulty neither can compete
With that wherein you navigate your feet.
As once George Gorham said of Pixley, so
I say of you: 'The prison yawns before you,
The turnkey stalks behind!' Now will you go?
Or lag, and let that functionary floor you?
To change the metaphor - you seem to be
Between Judge Wallace and the deep, deep sea!

Industrial Discontent
As time rolled on the whole world came to be
A desolation and a darksome curse;
And some one said: 'The changes that you see
In the fair frame of things, from bad to worse,
Are wrought by strikes. The sun withdrew his glimmer
Because the moon assisted with her shimmer.
'Then, when poor Luna, straining very hard,
Doubled her light to serve a darkling world,
He called her 'scab,' and meanly would retard
Her rising: and at last the villain hurled
A heavy beam which knocked her o'er the Lion
Into the nebula of great O'Ryan.
'The planets all had struck some time before,
Demanding what they said were equal rights:
Some pointing out that others had far more
That a fair dividend of satellites.
So all went out - though those the best provided,
If they had dared, would rather have abided.
'The stars struck too - I think it was because
The comets had more liberty than they,
And were not bound by any hampering laws,
While they were fixed; and there are those who say
The comets' tresses nettled poor Altair,
An aged orb that hasn't any hair.

'The earth's the only one that isn't in
The movement - I suppose because she's watched
With horror and disgust how her fair skin
Her pranking parasites have fouled and blotched
With blood and grease in every labor riot,
When seeing any purse or throat to fly at.'

Inspiration
O hoary sculptor, stay thy hand:
I fain would view the lettered stone.
What carvest thou? perchance some grand
And solemn fancy all thine own.
For oft to know the fitting word
Some humble worker God permits.
'Jain Ann Meginnis,
Agid 3rd.
He givith His beluved fits.'

Invocation
Goddess of Liberty! O thou
Whose tearless eyes behold the chain,
And look unmoved upon the slain,
Eternal peace upon thy brow,
Before thy shrine the races press,
Thy perfect favor to implore
The proudest tyrant asks no more,
The ironed anarchist no less.
Thine altar-coals that touch the lips
Of prophets kindle, too, the brand
By Discord flung with wanton hand
Among the houses and the ships.
Upon thy tranquil front the star
Burns bleak and passionless and white,
Its cold inclemency of light
More dreadful than the shadows are.
Thy name we do not here invoke
Our civic rites to sanctify:
Enthroned in thy remoter sky,
Thou heedest not our broken yoke.
Thou carest not for such as we:
Our millions die to serve the still
And secret purpose of thy will.
They perish - what is that to thee?
The light that fills the patriot's tomb
Is not of thee. The shining crown
Compassionately offered down
To those who falter in the gloom,

And fall, and call upon thy name,
And die desiring - 'tis the sign
Of a diviner love than thine,
Rewarding with a richer fame.
To him alone let freemen cry
Who hears alike the victor's shout,
The song of faith, the moan of doubt,
And bends him from his nearer sky.

God of my country and my race!
So greater than the gods of old
So fairer than the prophets told
Who dimly saw and feared thy face,
Who didst but half reveal thy will
And gracious ends to their desire,
Behind the dawn's advancing fire
Thy tender day-beam veiling still,
To whom the unceasing suns belong,
And cause is one with consequence,
To whose divine, inclusive sense
The moan is blended with the song,
Whose laws, imperfect and unjust,
Thy just and perfect purpose serve:
The needle, howsoe'er it swerve,
Still warranting the sailor's trust,
God, lift thy hand and make us free
To crown the work thou hast designed.
O, strike away the chains that bind
Our souls to one idolatry!
The liberty thy love hath given
We thank thee for. We thank thee for
Our great dead fathers' holy war
Wherein our manacles were riven.
We thank thee for the stronger stroke
Ourselves delivered and incurred
When - thine incitement half unheard
The chains we riveted we broke.
We thank thee that beyond the sea
Thy people, growing ever wise,
Turn to the west their serious eyes
And dumbly strive to be as we.
As when the sun's returning flame
Upon the Nileside statue shone,

And struck from the enchanted stone
The music of a mighty fame,
Let Man salute the rising day
Of Liberty, but not adore.
'Tis Opportunity - no more
A useful, not a sacred, ray.
It bringeth good, it bringeth ill,

As he possessing shall elect.
He maketh it of none effect
Who walketh not within thy will.
Give thou more or less, as we
Shall serve the right or serve the wrong.
Confirm our freedom but so long
As we are worthy to be free.
But when (O, distant be the time!)
Majorities in passion draw
Insurgent swords to murder Law,
And all the land is red with crime;
Or - nearer menace! when the band
Of feeble spirits cringe and plead
To the gigantic strength of Greed,
And fawn upon his iron hand;
Nay, when the steps to state are worn
In hollows by the feet of thieves,
And Mammon sits among the sheaves
And chuckles while the reapers mourn:
Then stay thy miracle! replace
The broken throne, repair the chain,
Restore the interrupted reign
And veil again thy patient face.
Lo! here upon the world's extreme
We stand with lifted arms and dare
By thine eternal name to swear
Our country, which so fair we deem

Upon whose hills, a bannered throng,
The spirits of the sun display
Their flashing lances day by day
And hear the sea's pacific song
Shall be so ruled in right and grace
That men shall say: 'O, drive afield
The lawless eagle from the shield,
And call an angel to the place!'

J.F.B.
How well this man unfolded to our view
The world's beliefs of Death and Heaven and
Hell This man whose own convictions none could tell,
Nor if his maze of reason had a clew.
Dogmas he wrote for daily bread, but knew
The fair philosophies of doubt so well
That while we listened to his words there fell
Some that were strangely comforting, though true.
Marking how wise we grew upon his doubt,
We said: 'If so, by groping in the night,
He can proclaim some certain paths of trust,

How great our profit if he saw about
His feet the highways leading to the light.'
Now he sees all. Ah, Christ! his mouth is dust!

James L. Flood
As oft it happens in the youth of day
That mists obscure the sun's imperfect ray,
Who, as he's mounting to the dome's extreme,
Smites and dispels them with a steeper beam,
So you the vapors that begirt your birth
Consumed, and manifested all your worth.
But still one early vice obstructs the light
And sullies all the visible and bright
Display of mind and character. You write.

Johndonkey
Thus the poor ass whose appetite has ne'er
Known than the thistle any sweeter fare
Thinks all the world eats thistles. Thus the clown,
The wit and Mentor of the country town,
Grins through the collar of a horse and thinks
Others for pleasure do as he for drinks,
Though secretly, because unwilling still
In public to attest their lack of skill.
Each dunce whose life and mind all follies mar
Believes as he is all men living are
His vices theirs, their understandings his;
Naught that he knows not, all he fancies, is.
How odd that any mind such stuff should boast!
How natural to write it in the Post!

Judex Judicatus
Judge Armstrong, when the poor have sought your aid,
To be released from vows that they have made
In haste, and leisurely repented, you,
As stern as Rhadamanthus (Minos too,
And AEeacus) have drawn your fierce brows down
And petrified them with a moral frown!
With iron-faced rigor you have made them run
The gauntlet of publicity - each Hun
Or Vandal of the public press allowed
To throw their households open to the crowd
And bawl their secret bickerings aloud.
When Wealth before you suppliant appears,
Bang! go the doors and open fly your ears!

The blinds are drawn, the lights diminished burn,
Lest eyes too curious should look and learn
That gold refines not, sweetens not a life
Of conjugal brutality and strife
That vice is vulgar, though it gilded shine
Upon the curve of a judicial spine.
The veiled complainant's whispered evidence,
The plain collusion and the no defense,
The sealed exhibits and the secret plea,
The unrecorded and unseen decree,
The midnight signature and - chink! chink! chink!
Nay, pardon, upright Judge, I did but think
I heard that sound abhorred of honest men;
No doubt it was the scratching of your pen.
O California! long-enduring land,
Where Judges fawn upon the Golden Hand,
Proud of such service to that rascal thing
As slaves would blush to render to a king
Judges, of judgment destitute and heart,
Of conscience conscious only by the smart
From the recoil (so insight is enlarged)
Of duty accidentally discharged;
Invoking still a 'song o' sixpence' from
The Scottish fiddle of each lusty palm,
Thy Judges, California, skilled to play
This silent music, through the livelong-day
Perform obsequious before the rich,
And still the more they scratch the more they itch!

Judgment

I drew aside the Future's veil
And saw upon his bier
The poet Whitman. Loud the wail
And damp the falling tear.
'He's dead - he is no more!' one cried,
With sobs of sorrow crammed;
'No more? He's this much more,' replied
Another: 'he is damned!'

Justice

Jack Doe met Dick Roe, whose wife he loved,
And said: 'I will get the best of him.'
So pulling a knife from his boot, he shoved
It up to the hilt in the breast of him.
Then he moved that weapon forth and back,
Enlarging the hole he had made with it,
Till the smoking liver fell out, and Jack

Merrily, merrily played with it.
Then he reached within and he seized the slack
Of the lesser bowel, and, traveling
Hither and thither, looked idly back
On that small intestine, raveling.
The wretched Richard, with many a grin
Laid on with exceeding suavity,
Curled up and died, and they ran John in
And charged him with sins of gravity.
The case was tried and a verdict found:
The jury, with great humanity,
Acquitted the prisoner on the ground
Of extemporary insanity.

L'audace

Daughter of God! Audacity divine
Of clowns the terror and of brains the sign
Not thou the inspirer of the rushing fool,
Not thine of idiots the vocal drool:
Thy bastard sister of the brow of brass,
Presumption, actuates the charging ass.
Sky-born Audacity! of thee who sings
Should strike with freer hand than mine the strings;
The notes should mount on pinions true and strong,
For thou, the subject shouldst sustain the song,
Till angels lean from Heaven, a breathless throng!
Alas! with reeling heads and wavering tails,
They (notes, not angels) dropp and the hymn fails;
The minstrel's tender fingers and his thumbs
Are torn to rags upon the lyre he strums.
Have done! the lofty thesis makes demand
For stronger voices and a harder hand:
Night-howling apes to make the notes aspire,
And Poet Riley's fist to slug the rebel wire!

Laus Lucis

Each to his taste: some men prefer to play
At mystery, as others at piquet.
Some sit in mystic meditation; some
Parade the street with tambourine and drum.
One studies to decipher ancient lore
Which, proving stuff, he studies all the more;
Another swears that learning is but good
To darken things already understood,
Then writes upon Simplicity so well
That none agree on what he wants to tell,
And future ages will declare his pen

Inspired by gods with messages to men.
To found an ancient order those devote
Their time - with ritual, regalia, goat,
Blankets for tossing, chairs of little ease
And all the modern inconveniences;
These, saner, frown upon unmeaning rites
And go to church for rational delights.
So all are suited, shallow and profound,
The prophets prosper and the world goes round.
For me - unread in the occult, I'm fain
To damn all mysteries alike as vain,
Spurn the obscure and base my faith upon
The Revelations of the good St. John.

Liberty

"Let there be Liberty!' God said, and, lo!
The red skies all were luminous. The glow
Struck first Columbia's kindling mountain peaks
One hundred and eleven years ago!'
So sang a patriot whom once I saw
Descending Bunker's holy hill. With awe
I noted that he shone with sacred light,
Like Moses with the tables of the Law.
One hundred and eleven years? O small
And paltry period compared with all
The tide of centuries that flowed and ebbed
To etch Yosemite's divided wall!
Ah, Liberty, they sing you always young
Whose harps are in your adoration strung
(Each swears you are his countrywoman, too,
And speak no language but his mother tongue).
And truly, lass, although with shout and horn
Man has all-hailed you from creation's morn,
I cannot think you old - I think, indeed,
You are by twenty centuries unborn.

Llewellen Powell

Villain, when the word is spoken,
And your chains at last are broken
When the gibbet's chilling shade
Ceases darkly to enfold you,
And the angel who enrolled you
As a master of the trade
Of assassination sadly
Blots the record he has made,
And your name and title paints
In the calendar of saints;

When the devils, dancing madly
In the midmost Hell, are very
Multitudinously merry
Then beware, beware, beware!
Nemesis is everywhere!
You shall hear her at your back,
And, your hunted visage turning,
Fancy that her eyes are burning
Like a tiger's on your track!
You shall hear her in the breeze
Whispering to summer trees.
You shall hear her calling, calling
To your spirit through the storm
When the giant billows form
And the splintered lightning, falling
Down the heights of Heaven, appalling,
Splendors all the tossing seas!
On your bed at night reclining,
Stars into your chamber shining
As they roll around the Pole,
None their purposes divining,
Shall appear to search your soul,
And to gild the mark of Cain
That burns into your tortured brain!
And the dead man's eyes shall ever
Meet your own wherever you,
Desperate, shall turn you to,
And you shall escape them never!
By your heritage of guilt;
By the blood that you have spilt;
By the Law that you have broken;
By the terrible red token
That you bear upon your brow;
By the awful sentence spoken
And irrevocable vow
Which consigns you to a living
Death and to the unforgiving
Furies who avenge your crime
Through the periods of time;
By that dread eternal doom
Hinted in your future's gloom,
As the flames infernal tell
Of their power and perfection
In their wavering reflection
On the battlements of Hell;
By the mercy you denied,
I condemn your guilty soul
In your body to abide,
Like a serpent in a hole!

Lucifer Of The Torch
O Reverend Ravlin, once with sounding lung
You shook the bloody banner of your tongue,
Urged all the fiery boycotters afield
And swore you'd rather follow them than yield,
Alas, how brief the time, how great the change!
Your dogs of war are ailing all of mange;
The loose leash dangles from your finger-tips,
But the loud 'havoc' dies upon your lips.
No spirit animates your feeble clay
You'd rather yield than even run away.
In vain McGlashan labors to inspire
Your pallid nostril with his breath of fire:
The light of battle's faded from your face
You keep the peace, John Chinaman his place.
O Ravlin, what cold water, thrown by whom
Upon the kindling Boycott's ruddy bloom,
Has slaked your parching blood-thirst and allayed
The flash and shimmer of your lingual blade?
Your salary - your salary's unpaid!
In the old days, when Christ with scourges drave
The Ravlins headlong from the Temple's nave,
Each bore upon his pelt the mark divine
The Boycott's red authenticating sign.
Birth-marked forever in surviving hurts,
Glowing and smarting underneath their shirts,
Successive Ravlins have revenged their shame
By blowing every coal and flinging flame.
And you, the latest (may you be the last!)
Endorsed with that hereditary, vast
And monstrous rubric, would the feud prolong,
Save that cupidity forbids the wrong.
In strife you preferably pass your days
But brawl no moment longer than it pays.
By shouting when no more you can incite
The dogs to put the timid sheep to flight
To load, for you, the brambles with their fleece,
You cackle concord to congenial geese,
Put pinches of goodwill upon their tails
And pluck them with a touch that never fails.

Lusus Politicus
Come in, old gentleman. How do you do?
Delighted, I'm sure, that you've called.
I'm a sociable sort of a chap and you
Are a pleasant appearing person, too,
With a head agreeably bald.
That's right - sit down in the scuttle of coal

And put up your feet in a chair.
It is better to have them there:
And I've always said that a hat of lead,
Such as I see you wear,
Was a better hat than a hat of glass.
And your boots of brass
Are a natural kind of boots, I swear.
'May you blow your nose on a paper of pins?'
Why, certainly, man, why not?
I rather expected you'd do it before,
When I saw you poking it in at the door.
It's dev'lish hot
The weather, I mean. 'You are twins'?
Why, that was evident at the start,
From the way that you paint your head
In stripes of purple and red,
With dots of yellow.
That proves you a fellow
With a love of legitimate art.
'You've bitten a snake and are feeling bad'?
That's very sad,
But Longfellow's words I beg to recall:
Your lot is the common lot of all.
'Horses are trees and the moon is a sneeze'?
That, I fancy, is just as you please.
Some think that way and others hold
The opposite view;
I never quite knew,
For the matter o' that,
When everything's been said
May I offer this mat
If you will stand on your head?
I suppose I look to be upside down
From your present point of view.
It's a giddy old world, from king to clown,
And a topsy-turvy, too.
But, worthy and now uninverted old man,
You're built, at least, on a normal plan
If ever a truth I spoke.
Smoke?
Your air and conversation
Are a liberal education,
And your clothes, including the metal hat
And the brazen boots - what's that?
'You never could stomach a Democrat
Since General Jackson ran?
You're another sort, but you predict
That your party'll get consummately licked?'
Good God! what a queer old man!

Mad

O ye who push and fight
To hear a wanton sing
Who utter the delight
That has the bogus ring,
O men mature in years,
In understanding young,
The membranes of whose ears
She tickles with her tongue,
O wives and daughters sweet,
Who call it love of art
To kiss a woman's feet
That crush a woman's heart,
O prudent dams and sires,
Your docile young who bring
To see how man admires
A sinner if she sing,
O husbands who impart
To each assenting spouse
The lesson that shall start
The buds upon your brows,
All whose applauding hands
Assist to rear the fame
That throws o'er all the lands
The shadow of its shame,
Go drag her car! the mud
Through which its axle rolls
Is partly human blood
And partly human souls.
Mad, mad! your senses whirl
Like devils dancing free,
Because a strolling girl
Can hold the note high C.
For this the avenging rod
Of Heaven ye dare defy,
And tear the law that God
Thundered from Sinai!

Magnanimity

'To the will of the people we loyally bow!'
That's the minority shibboleth now.
O noble antagonists, answer me flat
What would you do if you didn't do that?

Master Of Three Arts

Your various talents, Goldenson, command

Respect: you are a poet and can draw.
It is a pity that your gifted hand
Should ever have been raised against the law.
If you had drawn no pistol, but a picture,
You would have saved your throttle from a stricture.
About your poetry I'm not so sure:
'Tis certain we have much that's quite as bad,
Whose hardy writers have not to endure
The hangman's fondling. It is said they're mad:
Though lately Mr. Brooks (I mean the poet)
Looked well, and if demented didn't show it.
Well, Goldenson, I am a poet, too
Taught by the muses how to smite the harp
And lift the tuneful voice, although, like you
And Brooks, I sometimes flat and sometimes sharp.
But let me say, with no desire to taunt you,
I never murder even the girls I want to.
I hold it one of the poetic laws
To sing of life, not take. I've ever shown
A high regard for human life because
I have such trouble to support my own.
And you - well, you'll find trouble soon in blowing
Your private coal to keep it red and glowing.
I fancy now I see you at the Gate
Approach St. Peter, crawling on your belly,
You cry: 'Good sir, take pity on my state
Forgive the murderer of Mamie Kelly!'
And Peter says: 'O, that's all right - but, mister,
You scribbled rhymes. In Hell I'll make you blister!'

Matter For Gratitude

Be pleased, O Lord, to take a people's thanks
That Thine avenging sword has spared our ranks
That Thou hast parted from our lips the cup
And forced our neighbors' lips to drink it up.
Father of Mercies, with a heart contrite
We thank Thee that Thou goest south to smite,
And sparest San Francisco's loins, to crack
Thy lash on Hermosillo's bleeding back
That o'er our homes Thine awful angel spread
His wings in vain, and Guaymas weeps instead.
We praise Thee, God, that Yellow Fever here
His horrid banner has not dared to rear,
Consumption's jurisdiction to contest,
Her dagger deep in every second breast!
Catarrh and Asthma and Congestive Chill
Attest Thy bounty and perform Thy will.
These native messengers obey Thy call
They summon singly, but they summon all.

Not, as in Mexico's impested clime,
Can Yellow Jack commit recurring crime.
We thank Thee that Thou killest all the time.
Thy tender mercies, Father, never end:
Upon all heads Thy blessings still descend,
Though their forms vary. Here the sown seeds yield
Abundant grain that whitens all the field
There the smit corn stands barren on the plain,
Thrift reaps the straw and Famine gleans in vain.
Here the fat priest to the contented king
Points out the contrast and the people sing
There mothers eat their offspring. Well, at least
Thou hast provided offspring for the feast.
An earthquake here rolls harmless through the land,
And Thou art good because the chimneys stand
There templed cities sink into the sea,
And damp survivors, howling as they flee,
Skip to the hills and hold a celebration
In honor of Thy wise discrimination.
O God, forgive them all, from Stoneman down,
Thy smile who construe and expound Thy frown,
And fall with saintly grace upon their knees
To render thanks when Thou dost only sneeze.

Mendax

High Lord of Liars, Pickering, to thee
Let meaner mortals bend the subject knee!
Thine is mendacity's imperial crown,
Alike by genius, action and renown.
No man, since words could set a cheek aflame
E'er lied so greatly with so little shame!
O bad old man, must thy remaining years
Be passed in leading idiots by their ears
Thine own (which Justice, if she ruled the roast
Would fasten to the penitential post)
Still wagging sympathetically hung
the same rocking-bar that bears thy tongue?
Thou dog of darkness, dost thou hope to stay
Time's dread advance till thou hast had thy day?
Dost think the Strangler will release his hold
Because, forsooth, some fibs remain untold?
No, no - beneath thy multiplying load
Of years thou canst not tarry on the road
To dabble in the blood thy leaden feet
Have pressed from bosoms that have ceased to beat
Of reputations margining thy way,
Nor wander from the path new truth to slay.
Tell to thyself whatever lies thou wilt,
Catch as thou canst at pennies got by guilt

Straight down to death this blessed year thou'lt sink,
Thy life washed out as with a wave of ink.
But if this prophecy be not fulfilled,
And thou who killest patience be not killed;
If age assail in vain and vice attack
Only by folly to be beaten back;
Yet Nature can this consolation give:
The rogues who die not are condemned to live!

Metempsychosis

Once with Christ he entered Salem,
Once in Moab bullied Balaam,
Once by Apuleius staged
He the pious much enraged.
And, again, his head, as beaver,
Topped the neck of Nick the Weaver.
Omar saw him (minus tether
Free and wanton as the weather:
Knowing naught of bit or spur)
Stamping over Bahram-Gur.
Now, as Altgeld, see him joy
As Governor of Illinois!

Montague Leverson

As some enormous violet that towers
Colossal o'er the heads of lowlier flowers
Its giant petals royally displayed,
And casting half the landscape into shade;
Delivering its odors, like the blows
Of some strong slugger, at the public nose;
Pride of two Nations - for a single State
Would scarce suffice to sprout a plant so great;
So Leverson's humility, outgrown
The meaner virtues that he deigns to own,
To the high skies its great corolla rears,
O'ertopping all he has except his ears.

Montefiore

I saw—'t was in a dream, the other night
A man whose hair with age was thin and white;
One hundred years had bettered by his birth,
And still his step was firm, his eye was bright.
Before him and about him pressed a crowd.
Each head in reverence was bared and bowed,
And Jews and Gentiles in a hundred tongues

Extolled his deeds and spake his fame aloud.
I joined the throng and, pushing forward, cried,
"Montefiore!" with the rest, and vied
In efforts to caress the hand that ne'er
To want and worth had charity denied.
So closely round him swarmed our shouting clan
He scarce could breathe, and, taking from a pan
A gleaming coin, he tossed it o'er our heads,
And in a moment was a lonely man!

Mr. Fink's Debating Donkey
Of a person known as Peters I will humbly crave your leave
An unusual adventure into narrative to weave
Mr. William Perry Peters, of the town of Muscatel,
A public educator and an orator as well.
Mr. Peters had a weakness which, 'tis painful to relate,
Was a strong predisposition to the pleasures of debate.
He would foster disputation wheresoever he might be;
In polygonal contention none so happy was as he.
'Twas observable, however, that the exercises ran
Into monologue by Peters, that rhetorical young man.
And the Muscatelian rustics who assisted at the show,
By involuntary silence testified their overthrow
Mr. Peters, all unheedful of their silence and their grief,
Still effacing every vestige of erroneous belief.
O, he was a sore affliction to all heretics so bold
As to entertain opinions that he didn't care to hold.
One day - 't was in pursuance of a pedagogic plan
For the mental elevation of Uncultivated Man
Mr. Peters, to his pupils, in dismissing them, explained
That the Friday evening following (unless, indeed, it rained)
Would be signalized by holding in the schoolhouse a debate
Free to all who their opinions might desire to ventilate
On the question, 'Which is better, as a serviceable gift,
Speech or hearing, from barbarity the human mind to lift?'
The pupils told their fathers, who, forehanded always, met
At the barroom to discuss it every evening, dry or wet,
They argued it and argued it and spat upon the stove,
And the non-committal 'barkeep' on their differences throve.
And I state it as a maxim in a loosish kind of way:
You'll have the more to back your word the less you have to say.
Public interest was lively, but one Ebenezer Fink
Of the Rancho del Jackrabbit, only seemed to sit and think.
On the memorable evening all the men of Muscatel
Came to listen to the logic and the eloquence as well
All but William Perry Peters, whose attendance there, I fear.
Was to wreak his ready rhetoric upon the public ear,
And prove (whichever side he took) that hearing wouldn't lift
The human mind as ably as the other, greater gift.

The judges being chosen and the disputants enrolled,
The question he proceeded in extenso to unfold:
'Resolved - The sense of hearing lifts the mind up out of reach
Of the fogs of error better than the faculty of speech.'
This simple proposition he expounded, word by word,
Until they best understood it who least perfectly had heard.
Even the judges comprehended as he ventured to explain
The impact of a spit-ball admonishing in vain.
Beginning at a period before Creation's morn,
He had reached the bounds of tolerance and Adam yet unborn.
As down the early centuries of pre-historic time
He tracked important principles and quoted striking rhyme,
And Whisky Bill, prosaic soul! proclaiming him a jay,
Had risen and like an earthquake, 'reeled unheededly away,'
And a late lamented cat, when opportunity should serve,
Was preparing to embark upon her parabolic curve,
A noise arose outside - the door was opened with a bang
And old Ebenezer Fink was heard ejaculating 'G'lang!'
Straight into that assembly gravely marched without a wink
An ancient ass - the property it was of Mr. Fink.
Its ears depressed and beating time to its infestive tread,
Silent through silence moved amain that stately quadruped!
It stopped before the orator, and in the lamplight thrown
Upon its tail they saw that member weighted with a stone.
Then spake old Ebenezer: 'Gents, I heern o' this debate
On w'ether v'ice or y'ears is best the mind to elevate.
Now 'yer's a bird ken throw some light uponto that tough theme:
He has 'em both, I'm free to say, oncommonly extreme.
He wa'n't invited for to speak, but he will not refuse
(If t'other gentleman ken wait) to exposay his views.'
Ere merriment or anger o'er amazement could prevail;
He cut the string that held the stone on that canary's tail.
Freed from the weight, that member made a gesture of delight,
Then rose until its rigid length was horizontal quite.
With lifted head and level ears along his withers laid,
Jack sighed, refilled his lungs and then - to put it mildly, brayed!
He brayed until the stones were stirred in circumjacent hills,
And sleeping women rose and fled, in divers kinds of frills.
'T is said that awful bugle-blast - to make the story brief
Wafted William Perry Peters through the window, like a leaf!
Such is the tale. If anything additional occurred
'Tis not set down, though, truly, I remember to have heard
That a gentleman named Peters, now residing at Soquel,
A considerable distance from the town of Muscatel,
Is opposed to education, and to rhetoric, as well.

Mr. Sheets
The Devil stood before the gate
Of Heaven. He had a single mate:

Behind him, in his shadow, slunk
Clay Sheets in a perspiring funk.
'Saint Peter, see this season ticket,'
Said Satan; 'pray undo the wicket.'
The sleepy Saint threw slight regard
Upon the proffered bit of card,
Signed by some clerical dead-beats:
'Admit the bearer and Clay Sheets.'
Peter expanded all his eyes:
"Clay Sheets?' well, I'll be damned!' he cries.
'Our couches are of golden cloud;
Nothing of earth is here allowed.
I'll let you in,' he added, shedding
On Nick a smile 'but not your bedding.'

My Lord Poet

'Who drives fat oxen should himself be fat;'
Who sings for nobles, he should noble be.
There's no non sequitur, I think, in that,
And this is logic plain as a, b, c.
Now, Hector Stuart, you're a Scottish prince,
If right you fathom your descent - that fall
From grace; and since you have no peers, and since
You have no kind of nobleness at all,
'Twere better to sing little, lest you wince
When made by heartless critics to sing small.
And yet, my liege, I bid you not despair
Ambition conquers but a realm at once:
For European bays arrange your hair
Two continents, in time, shall crown you Dunce!

My Monument

It is pleasant to think, as I'm watching my ink
A-drying along my paper,
That a monument fine will surely be mine
When death has extinguished my taper.
From each rhyming scribe of the journalist tribe
Purged clean of all sentiments narrow,
A pebble will mark his respect for the stark
Stiff body that's under the barrow.
By fellow-bards thrown, thus stone upon stone
Will make my celebrity deathless.
O, I wish I could think, as I gaze at my ink,
They'd wait till my carcass is breathless.

Nanine

We heard a song-bird trilling
'T was but a night ago.
Such rapture he was rilling
As only we could know.
This morning he is flinging
His music from the tree,
But something in the singing
Is not the same to me.
His inspiration fails him,
Or he has lost his skill.
Nanine, Nanine, what ails him
That he should sing so ill?
Nanine is not replying
She hears no earthly song.
The sun and bird are lying
And the night is, O, so long!

Nimrod

There were brave men, some one has truly said,
Before Atrides (those were mostly dead
Behind him) and ere you could e'er occur
Actaeon lived, Nimrod and Bahram-Gur.
In strength and speed and daring they excelled:
The stag they overtook, the lion felled.
Ah, yes, great hunters flourished before you,
And for Munchausen lived great talkers too.
There'll be no more; there's much to kill, but - well,
You have left nothing in the world to tell!

Not Guilty

'I saw your charms in another's arms,'
Said a Grecian swain with his blood a-boil;
'And he kissed you fair as he held you there,
A willing bird in a serpent's coil!'
The maid looked up from the cinctured cup
Wherein she was crushing the berries red,
Pain and surprise in her honest eyes
'It was only one o' those gods,' she said.

Novum Organum

In Bacon see the culminating prime
Of Anglo-Saxon intellect and crime.
He dies and Nature, settling his affairs,
Parts his endowments among us, his heirs:

To every one a pinch of brain for seed,
And, to develop it, a pinch of greed.
Each thrifty heir, to make the gift suffice,
Buries the talent to manure the vice.

Omnes Vanitas
Alas for ambition's possessor!
Alas for the famous and proud!
The Isle of Manhattan's best dresser
Is wearing a hand-me-down shroud.
The world has forgotten his glory;
The wagoner sings on his wain,
And Chauncey Depew tells a story,
And jackasses laugh in the lane.

On A Proposed Crematory
When a fair bridge is builded o'er the gulf
Between two cities, some ambitious fool,
Hot for distinction, pleads for earliest leave
To push his clumsy feet upon the span,
That men in after years may single him,
Saying: 'Behold the fool who first went o'er!'
So be it when, as now the promise is,
Next summer sees the edifice complete
Which some do name a crematorium,
Within the vantage of whose greater maw's
Quicker digestion we shall cheat the worm
And circumvent the handed mole who loves,
With tunnel, adit, drift and roomy stope,
To mine our mortal parts in all their dips
And spurs and angles. Let the fool stand forth
To link his name with this fair enterprise,
As first decarcassed by the flame. And if
With rival greedings for the fiery fame
They push in clamoring multitudes, or if
With unaccustomed modesty they all
Hold off, being something loth to qualify,
Let me select the fittest for the rite.
By heaven! I'll make so warrantable, wise
And excellent censure of their true deserts,
And such a searching canvass of their claims,
That none shall bait the ballot. I'll spread my choice
Upon the main and general of those
Who, moved of holy impulse, pulpit-born,
Protested 'twere a sacrilege to burn
God's gracious images, designed to rot,
And bellowed for the right of way for each

Distempered carrion through the water pipes.
With such a sturdy, boisterous exclaim
They did discharge themselves from their own throats
Against the splintered gates of audience
'Twere wholesomer to take them in at mouth
Than ear. These shall burn first: their ignible
And seasoned substances - trunks, legs and arms,
Blent indistinguishable in a mass,
Like winter-woven serpents in a pit
None vantaged of his fellow-fools in point
Of precedence, and all alive shall serve
As fueling to fervor the retort
For after cineration of true men.

On Stone
As in a dream, strange epitaphs I see,
Inscribed on yet unquarried stone,
Where wither flowers yet unstrown
The Campo Santo of the time to be.

On The Platform
When Dr. Bill Bartlett stepped out of the hum
Of Mammon's distracting and wearisome strife
To stand and deliver a lecture on 'Some
Conditions of Intellectual Life,'
I cursed the offender who gave him the hall
To lecture on any conditions at all!
But he rose with a fire divine in his eye,
Haranguing with endless abundance of breath,
Till I slept; and I dreamed of a gibbet reared high,
And Dr. Bill Bartlett was dressing for death.
And I thought in my dream: 'These conditions, no doubt,
Are bad for the life he was talking about.'
So I cried (pray remember this all was a dream):
'Get off of the platform! it isn't the kind!'
But he fell through the trap, with a jerk at the beam,
And wiggled his toes to unburden his mind.
And, O, so bewitching the thoughts he advanced,
That I clung to his ankles, attentive, entranced!

On The Wedding Of An Aeronaut
Aeronaut, you're fairly caught,
Despite your bubble's leaven:
Out of the skies a lady's eyes
Have brought you down to Heaven!

No more, no more you'll freely soar
Above the grass and gravel:
Henceforth you'll walk - and she will chalk
The line that you're to travel!

One And One Are Two

The trumpet sounded and the dead
Came forth from earth and ocean,
And Pickering arose and sped
Aloft with wobbling motion.
'What makes him fly lop-sided?' cried
A soul of the elected.
'One ear was wax,' a rogue replied,
'And isn't resurrected.'
Below him on the pitted plain,
By his abandoned hollow,
His hair and teeth tried all in vain
The rest of him to follow.
Saint Peter, seeing him ascend,
Came forward to the wicket,
And said: 'My mutilated friend,
I'll thank you for your ticket.'
'The Call,' said Pickering, his hand
To reach the latch extended.
Said Peter, affable and bland:
'The free-list is suspended
'What claim have you that's valid here?'
That ancient vilifier
Reflected; then, with look austere,
Replied: 'I am a liar.'
Said Peter: 'That is simple, neat
And candid Anglo-Saxon,
But - well, come in, and take a seat
Up there by Colonel Jackson.'

One Judge

Wallace, created on a noble plan
To show us that a Judge can be a Man;
Through moral mire exhaling mortal stench
God guided sweet and foot - clean to the Bench;
In salutation here and sign I lift
A hand as free as yours from lawless thrift,
A heart - ah, would I truly could proclaim
My bosom lighted with so pure a flame!
Alas, not love of justice moves my pen
To praise, or to condemn, my fellow men.
Good will and ill its busy point incite:

I do but gratify them when I write.
In palliation, though, I'd humbly state,
I love the righteous and the wicked hate.
So, sir, although we differ we agree,
Our work alike from persecution free,
And Heaven, approving you, consents to me.
Take, therefore, from this not all useless hand
The crown of honor - not in all the land
One honest man dissenting from the choice,
Nor in approval one Fred. Crocker's voice!

One Mood's Expression
See, Lord, fanatics all arrayed
For revolution!
To foil their villainous crusade
Unsheathe again the sacred blade
Of persecution.
What though through long disuse 't is grown
A trifle rusty?
'Gainst modern heresy, whose bone
Is rotten, and the flesh fly-blown,
It still is trusty.
Of sterner stuff thine ancient foes,
Unapprehensive,
Sprang forth to meet thy biting blows;
Our zealots chiefly to the nose
Assume the offensive.
Then wield the blade their necks to hack,
Nor ever spare one.
Thy crowns of martyrdom unpack,
But see that every martyr lack
The head to wear one.

One Morning
Because that I am weak, my love, and ill,
I cannot follow the impatient feet
Of my desire, but sit and watch the beat
Of the unpitying pendulum fulfill
The hour appointed for the air to thrill
And brighten at your coming. O my sweet,
The tale of moments is at last complete
The tryst is broken on the gusty hill!
O lady, faithful footed, loyal-eyed,
The long leagues silence me; yet doubt me not;
Think rather that the clock and sun have lied
And all too early, you have sought the spot.
For lo! despair has darkened all the light,

And till I see your face it still is night.

One Of The Redeemed
Saint Peter, standing at the Gate, beheld
A soul whose body Death had lately felled.
A pleasant soul as ever was, he seemed:
His step was joyous and his visage beamed.
'Good morning, Peter.' There was just a touch
Of foreign accent, but not overmuch.
The Saint bent gravely, like a stately tree,
And said: 'You have the advantage, sir, of me.'
'Renan of Paris,' said the immortal part
'A master of the literary art.
'I'm somewhat famous, too, I grieve to tell,
As controversialist and infidel.'
'That's of no consequence,' the Saint replied,
'Why, I myself my Master once denied.
'No one up here cares anything for that.
But is there nothing you were always at?
'It seems to me you were accused one day
Of something - what it was I can't just say.'
'Quite likely,' said the other; 'but I swear
My life was irreproachable and fair.'
Just then a soul appeared upon the wall,
Singing a hymn as loud as he could bawl.
About his head a golden halo gleamed,
As well befitted one of the redeemed.
A harp he bore and vigorously thumbed,
Strumming he sang, and, singing, ever strummed.
His countenance, suffused with holy pride,
Glowed like a pumpkin with a light inside.
'Ah! that's the chap,' said Peter, 'who declares:
'Renan's a rake and drunkard - smokes and swears.'
'Yes, that's the fellow - he's a preacher came
From San Francisco. Mansfield was his name.'
'Do you believe him?' said Renan. 'Great Scott!
Believe? Believe the blackguard? Of course not!
'Just walk right in and make yourself at home.

And if he pecks at you I'll cut his comb.
'He's only here because the Devil swore
He wouldn't have him, for the smile he wore.'
Resting his eyes one moment on that proof
Of saving grace, the Frenchman turned aloof,
And stepping down from cloud to cloud, said he:
'Thank you, monsieur, I'll see if he'll have me.'

One Of The Saints

Big Smith is an Oakland School Board man,
And he looks as good as ever he can;
And he's such a cold and a chaste Big Smith
That snowflakes all are his kin and kith.
Wherever his eye he chances to throw
The crystals of ice begin to grow;
And the fruits and flowers he sees are lost
By the singeing touch of a sudden frost.
The women all shiver whenever he's near,
And look upon us with a look austere
Effect of the Smithian atmosphere.
Such, in a word, is the moral plan
Of the Big, Big Smith, the School Board man.
When told that Madame Ferrier had taught
Hernani in school, his fist he brought
Like a trip-hammer down on his bulbous knee,
And he roared: 'Her Nanny? By gum, we'll see
If the public's time she dares devote
To the educatin' of any dam goat!'
'You do not entirely comprehend
Hernani's a play,' said his learned friend,
'By Victor Hugo - immoral and bad.
What's worse, it's French!' 'Well, well, my lad,'
Said Smith, 'if he cuts a swath so wide
I'll have him took re'glar up and tried!'
And he smiled so sweetly the other chap
Thought that himself was a Finn or Lapp
Caught in a storm of his native snows,
With a purple ear and an azure nose.
The Smith continued: 'I never pursue
Immoral readin'.' And that is true:
He's a saint of remarkably high degree,
With a mind as chaste as a mind can be;
But read! the devil a word can he!

One Of The Unfair Sex

She stood at the ticket-seller's
Serenely removing her glove,
While hundreds of strugglers and yellers,
And some that were good at a shove,
Were clustered behind her like bats in
a cave and unwilling to speak their love.
At night she still stood at that window
Endeavoring her money to reach;
The crowds right and left, how they sinned
O, How dreadfully sinned in their speech!
Ten miles either way they extended
their lines, the historians teach.

She stands there to-day legislation
Has failed to remove her. The trains
No longer pull up at that station;
And over the ghastly remains
Of the army that waited and died of
old age fall the snows and the rains.

One President

'What are those, father?' 'Statesmen, my child
Lacrymose, unparliamentary, wild.'
'What are they that way for, father?' 'Last fall,
'Our candidate's better,' they said, 'than all!''
'What did they say he was, father?' 'A man
Built on a straight incorruptible plan
Believing that none for an office would do
Unless he were honest and capable too.'
'Poor gentlemen - so disappointed!' 'Yes, lad,
That is the feeling that's driving them mad;
They're weeping and wailing and gnashing because
They find that he's all that they said that he was.'

Oneiromancy

I fell asleep and dreamed that I
Was flung, like Vulcan, from the sky;
Like him was lamed - another part:
His leg was crippled and my heart.
I woke in time to see my love
Conceal a letter in her glove

Ornithanthropos

'Let John P. Irish rise!' the edict rang
As when Creation into being sprang!
Nature, not clearly understanding, tried
To make a bird that on the air could ride.
But naught could baffle the creative plan
Despite her efforts 'twas almost a man.
Yet he had risen - to the bird a twin
Had she but fixed a wing upon his chin.

Over The Border

O, justice, you have fled, to dwell
In Mexico, unstrangled,
Lest you should hang as high as well,

As Haman dangled.
(I know not if his cord he twanged,
Or the King proved forgiving.
'Tis hard to think of Haman hanged,
And Haymond living.)
Yes, as I said: in mortal fear
To Mexico you journeyed;
For you were on your trial here,
And ill attorneyed.
The Law had long regarded you
As an extreme offender.
Religion looked upon you, too,
With thoughts untender.
The Press to you was cold as snow,
For sin you'd always call so.
In Politics you were de trop,
In Morals also.
All this is accurately true
And, faith! there might be more said;
But - well, to save your thrapple you
Fled, as aforesaid.
You're down in Mexico - that's plain
As that the sun is risen;
For Daniel Burns, down there, his chain
Drags round in prison.

Peace
When lion and lamb have together lain down
Spectators cry out, all in chorus;
'The lamb doesn't shrink nor the lion frown
A miracle's working before us!'
But 't is patent why Hot-head his wrath holds in,
And Faint-heart her terror and loathing;
For the one's but an ass in a lion's skin,
The other a wolf in sheep's clothing.

'Phil' Crimmins
Still as he climbed into the public view
His charms of person more apparent grew,
Till the pleased world that watched his airy grace
Saw nothing of him but his nether face
Forgot his follies with his head's retreat,
And blessed his virtues as it viewed their seat.

Philosopher Bimm

Republicans think Jonas Bimm
A Democrat gone mad,
And Democrats consider him
Republican and bad.
The Tough reviles him as a Dude
And gives it him right hot;
The Dude condemns his crassitude
And calls him sans culottes.
Derided as an Anglophile
By Anglophobes, forsooth,
As Anglophobe he feels, the while,
The Anglophilic tooth.
The Churchman calls him Atheist;
The Atheists, rough-shod,
Have ridden o'er him long and hissed
'The wretch believes in God!'
The Saints whom clergymen we call
Would kill him if they could;
The Sinners (scientists and all)
Complain that he is good.
All men deplore the difference
Between themselves and him,
And all devise expedients
For paining Jonas Bimm.
I too, with wild demoniac glee,
Would put out both his eyes;
For Mr. Bimm appears to me
Insufferably wise!

Piety

The pig is taught by sermons and epistles
To think the God of Swine has snout and bristles.
Judibras.

Poesy

Successive bards pursue Ambition's fire
That shines, Oblivion, above thy mire.
The latest mounts his predecessor's trunk,
And sinks his brother ere himself is sunk.
So die ingloriously Fame's elite,
But dams of dunces keep the line complete.

Political Economy

'I beg you to note,' said a Man to a Goose,
As he plucked from her bosom the plumage all loose,

'That pillows and cushions of feathers and beds
As warm as maids' hearts and as soft as their heads,
Increase of life's comforts the general sum
Which raises the standard of living.' 'Come, come,'
The Goose said, impatiently, 'tell me or cease,
How that is of any advantage to geese.'
'What, what!' said the man - 'you are very obtuse!
Consumption no profit to those who produce?
No good to accrue to Supply from a grand
Progressive expansion, all round, of Demand?
Luxurious habits no benefit bring
To those who purvey the luxurious thing?
Consider, I pray you, my friend, how the growth
Of luxury promises 'Promises,' quoth
The sufferer, 'what? to what course is it pledged
To pay me for being so often defledged?'
'Accustomed' - this notion the plucker expressed
As he ripped out a handful of down from her breast
'To one kind of luxury, people soon yearn
For others and ever for others in turn;
And the man who to-night on your feathers will rest,
His mutton or bacon or beef to digest,
His hunger to-morrow will wish to assuage
By dining on goose with a dressing of sage.'

Politics
That land full surely hastens to its end
Where public sycophants in homage bend
The populace to flatter, and repeat
The doubled echoes of its loud conceit.
Lowly their attitude but high their aim,
They creep to eminence through paths of shame,
Till, fixed securely in the seats of pow'r,
The dupes they flattered they at last devour.

Polyphemus
Twas a sick young man with a face ungay
And an eye that was all alone;
And he shook his head in a hopeless way
As he sat on a roadside stone.
'O, ailing youth, what untoward fate
Has made the sun to set
On your mirth and eye?' 'I'm constrained to state
I'm an ex-West Point cadet.
''Twas at cannon practice I got my hurt
And my present frame of mind;
For the gun went off with a double spurt

Before it, and also behind!'
'How sad, how sad, that a fine young chap,
When studying how to kill,
Should meet with so terrible a mishap
Precluding eventual skill.
'Ah, woful to think that a weapon made
For mowing down the foe
Should commit so dreadful an escapade
As to turn about to mow!'
No more he heeded while I condoled:
He was wandering in his mind;
His lonely eye unconsidered rolled,
And his views he thus defined:
"Twas O for a breach of the peace - 'twas O
For an international brawl!
But a piece of the breech - ah no, ah no,
I didn't want that at all.'

Posterity's Award

I'd long been dead, but I returned to earth.
Some small affairs posterity was making
A mess of, and I came to see that worth
Received its dues. I'd hardly finished waking,
The grave-mould still upon me, when my eye
Perceived a statue standing straight and high.
'Twas a colossal figure - bronze and gold
Nobly designed, in attitude commanding.
A toga from its shoulders, fold on fold,
Fell to the pedestal on which 'twas standing.
Nobility it had and splendid grace,
And all it should have had - except a face!
It showed no features: not a trace nor sign
Of any eyes or nose could be detected
On the smooth oval of its front no line
Where sites for mouths are commonly selected.
All blank and blind its faulty head it reared.
Let this be said: 'twas generously eared.
Seeing these things, I straight began to guess
For whom this mighty image was intended.
'The head,' I cried, 'is Upton's, and the dress
Is Parson Bartlett's own.' True, his cloak ended
Flush with his lowest vertebra, but no
Sane sculptor ever made a toga so.
Then on the pedestal these words I read:
'Erected Eighteen Hundred Ninety-seven'
(Saint Christofer! how fast the time had sped!
Of course it naturally does in Heaven)
'To --' (here a blank space for the name began)
'The Nineteenth Century's Great Foremost Man!'

'Completed' the inscription ended, 'in
The Year Three Thousand' - which was just arriving.
By Jove! thought I, 'twould make the founders grin
To learn whose fame so long has been surviving
To read the name posterity will place
In that blank void, and view the finished face.
Even as I gazed, the year Three Thousand came,
And then by acclamation all the people
Decreed whose was our century's best fame;
Then scaffolded the statue like a steeple,
To make the likeness; and the name was sunk
Deep in the pedestal's metallic trunk.
Whose was it? Gentle reader, pray excuse
The seeming rudeness, but I can't consent to
Be so forehanded with important news.

'Twas neither yours nor mine - let that content you.
If not, the name I must surrender, which,
Upon a dead man's word, was George K. Fitch!

Prayer

Fear not in any tongue to call
Upon the Lord - He's skilled in all.
But if He answereth my plea
He speaketh one unknown to me.

Presentiment

With saintly grace and reverent tread
She walked among the graves with me;
Her every footfall seemed to be
A benediction on the dead.
The guardian spirit of the place
She seemed, and I some ghost forlorn,
Surprised by the untimely morn
She made with her resplendent face.
Moved by some waywardness of will,
Three paces from the path apart
She stepped and stood—my prescient heart
Was stricken with a passing chill.
My child-lore of the years agone
Remembering, I smiled and thought,
"Who shudders suddenly at naught,
His grave is being trod upon."
But now I know that it was more
Than idle fancy. O, my sweet,
I did not know such little feet
Could make a buried heart so sore!

Psychographs
Says Gerald Massey: 'When I write, a band
Of souls of the departed guides my hand.'
How strange that poems cumbering our shelves,
Penned by immortal parts, have none themselves

Rebuke
When Admonition's hand essays
Our greed to curse,
Its lifted finger oft displays
Our missing purse.

Re-Edified
Lord of the tempest, pray refrain
From leveling this church again.
Now in its doom, as so you've willed it,
We acquiesce. But you'll rebuild it.

Rejected
When Dr. Charles O'Donnell died
They sank a box with him inside.
The plate with his initials three
Was simply graven - 'C.O.D.'
That night two demons of the Pit
Adown the coal-hole shunted it.
Ten million million leagues it fell,
Alighting at the gate of Hell.
Nick looked upon it with surprise,
A night-storm darkening his eyes.
'They've sent this rubbish, C.O.D.
I'll never pay a cent!' said he.

Religion
Hassan Bedreddin, clad in rags, ill-shod,
Sought the great temple of the living God.
The worshippers arose and drove him forth,
And one in power beat him with a rod.
'Allah,' he cried, 'thou seest what I got;
Thy servants bar me from the sacred spot.'
'Be comforted,' the Holy One replied;

'It is the only place where I am not.'

Religious Progress

Professor dear, I think it queer
That all these good religions
('Twixt you and me, some two or three
Are schemes for plucking pigeons)
I mean 'tis strange that every change
Our poor minds to unfetter
Entails a new religion - true
As t' other one, and better.
From each in turn the truth we learn,
That wood or flesh or spirit
May justly boast it rules the roast
Until we cease to fear it.
Nay, once upon a time long gone
Man worshipped Cat and Lizard:
His God he'd find in any kind
Of beast, from a to izzard.
When risen above his early love
Of dirt and blood and slumber,
He pulled down these vain deities,
And made one out of lumber.
'Far better that than even a cat,'
The Howisons all shouted;
'When God is wood religion's good!'
But one poor cynic doubted.
'A timber God - that's very odd!'
Said Progress, and invented
The simple plan to worship Man,
Who, kindly soul! consented.
But soon our eye we lift asky,
Our vows all unregarded,
And find (at least so says the priest)
The Truth and Man's discarded.
Along our line of march recline
Dead gods devoid of feeling;
And thick about each sun-cracked lout
Dried Howisons are kneeling.

Reminded

Beneath my window twilight made
Familiar mysteries of shade.
Faint voices from the darkening down
Were calling vaguely to the town.
Intent upon a low, far gleam
That burned upon the world's extreme,

I sat, with short reprieve from grief,
And turned the volume, leaf by leaf,
Wherein a hand, long dead, had wrought
A million miracles of thought.
My fingers carelessly unclung
The lettered pages, and among
Them wandered witless, nor divined
The wealth in which, poor fools, they mined.
The soul that should have led their quest
Was dreaming in the level west,
Where a tall tower, stark and still,
Uplifted on a distant hill,
Stood lone and passionless to claim
Its guardian star's returning flame.
I know not how my dream was broke,
But suddenly my spirit woke
Filled with a foolish fear to look
Upon the hand that clove the book,
Significantly pointing; next
I bent attentive to the text,
And read - and as I read grew old
The mindless words: 'Poor Tom's a-cold!'
Ah me! to what a subtle touch
The brimming cup resigns its clutch
Upon the wine. Dear God, is 't writ
That hearts their overburden bear
Of bitterness though thou permit
The pranks of Chance, alurk in nooks,
And striking coward blows from books,
And dead hands reaching everywhere?

Revenge

A spitcat sate on a garden gate
And a snapdog fared beneath;
Careless and free was his mien, and he
Held a fiddle-string in his teeth.
She marked his march, she wrought an arch
Of her back and blew up her tail;
And her eyes were green as ever were seen,
And she uttered a woful wail.
The spitcat's plaint was as follows:
'It ain't That I am to music a foe;
For fiddle-strings bide in my own inside,
And I twang them soft and low.
'But that dog has trifled with art and rifled
A kitten of mine, ah me!
That catgut slim was marauded from him:
'Tis the string that men call E.'
Then she sounded high, in the key of Y,

A note that cracked the tombs;
And the missiles through the firmament flew
From adjacent sleeping-rooms.
As her gruesome yell from the gate-post fell
She followed it down to earth;
And that snapdog wears a placard that bears
The inscription: 'Blind from birth.'

Rimer

The rimer quenches his unheeded fires,
The sound surceases and the sense expires.
Then the domestic dog, to east and west,
Expounds the passions burning in his breast.
The rising moon o'er that enchanted land
Pauses to hear and yearns to understand.

Safety-Clutch

Once I seen a human ruin
In a elevator - well.
And his members was bestrewin'
All the place where he had fell.
And I says, apostrophisin'
That uncommon woful wreck:
'Your position's so surprisin'
That I tremble for your neck!'
Then that ruin, smilin' sadly
And impressive, up and spoke:
'Well, I wouldn't tremble badly,
For it's been a fortnight broke.'
Then, for further comprehension
Of his attitude, he begs
I will focus my attention
On his various arms and legs
How they all are contumacious;
Where they each, respective, lie;
How one trotter proves ungracious,
T' other one an alibi.
These particulars is mentioned
For to show his dismal state,
Which I wasn't first intentioned
To specifical relate.
None is worser to be dreaded
That I ever have heard tell
Than the gent's who there was spreaded
In that elevator - well.
Now this tale is allegoric
It is figurative all,

For the well is metaphoric
And the feller didn't fall.
I opine it isn't moral
For a writer - man to cheat,
And despise to wear a laurel
As was gotten by deceit.
For 'tis Politics intended
By the elevator, mind,
It will boost a person splendid
If his talent is the kind.
Col. Bryan had the talent
(For the busted man is him)
And it shot him up right gallant
Till his head began to swim.
Then the rope it broke above him
And he painful came to earth
Where there's nobody to love him
For his detrimented worth.
Though he's living' none would know him,
Or at leastwise not as such.
Moral of this woful poem:
Frequent oil your safety clutch.

Salvini In America

Come, gentlemen - your gold.
Thanks: welcome to the show.
To hear a story told
In words you do not know.
Now, great Salvini, rise
And thunder through your tears,
Aha! friends, let your eyes
Interpret to your ears.
Gods! 't is a goodly game.
Observe his stride - how grand!
When legs like his declaim
Who can misunderstand?
See how that arm goes round.
It says, as plain as day:
'I love,' 'The lost is found,'
'Well met, sir,' or, 'Away!'
And mark the drawing down
Of brows. How accurate
The language of that frown:
Pain, gentlemen - or hate.
Those of the critic trade
Swear it is all as clear
As if his tongue were made
To fit an English ear.
Hear that Italian phrase!

Greek to your sense, 't is true;
But shrug, expression, gaze
Well, they are Grecian too.
But it is Art! God wot
Its tongue to all is known.
Faith! he to whom 't were not
Would better hold his own.
Shakespeare says act and word
Must match together true.
From what you've seen and heard,
How can you doubt they do?
Enchanting drama! Mark
The crowd 'from pit to dome',
One box alone is dark
The prompter stays at home.
Stupendous artist! You
Are lord of joy and woe:
We thrill if you say 'Boo,'
And thrill if you say 'Bo.'

Samuel Shortridge
Like a worn mother he attempts in vain
To still the unruly Crier of his brain:
The more he rocks the cradle of his chin
The more uproarious grows the brat within.

Sires And Sons
Wild wanton Luxury lays waste the land
With difficulty tilled by Thrift's hard hand!
Then dies the State! and, in its carcass found,
The millionaires, all maggot-like, abound.
Alas! was it for this that Warren died,
And Arnold sold himself to t' other side,
Stark piled at Bennington his British dead,
And Gates at Camden, Lee at Monmouth, fled?
For this that Perry did the foeman fleece,
And Hull surrender to preserve the peace?
Degenerate countrymen, renounce, I pray,
The slothful ease, the luxury, the gay
And gallant trappings of this idle life,
And be more fit for one another's wife.

Something In The Papers
'What's in the paper?' Oh, it's dev'lish dull:
There's nothing happening at all - a lull

After the war-storm. Mr. Someone's wife
Killed by her lover with, I think, a knife.
A fire on Blank Street and some babies - one,
Two, three or four, I don't remember, done
To quite a delicate and lovely brown.
A husband shot by woman of the town
The same old story. Shipwreck somewhere south.
The crew, all saved - or lost. Uncommon drouth
Makes hundreds homeless up the River Mud
Though, come to think, I guess it was a flood.
'T is feared some bank will burst - or else it won't
They always burst, I fancy - or they don't;
Who cares a cent? the banker pays his coin
And takes his chances: bullet in the groin
But that's another item - suicide
Fool lost his money (serve him right) and died.
Heigh-ho! there's noth Jerusalem! what's this:
Tom Jones has failed! My God, what an abyss
Of ruin! owes me seven hundred clear!
Was ever such a damned disastrous year!

Stephen Dorsey
Fly, heedless stranger, from this spot accurst,
Where rests in Satan an offender first
In point of greatness, as in point of time,
Of new-school rascals who proclaim their crime.
Skilled with a frank loquacity to blab
The dark arcana of each mighty grab,
And famed for lying from his early youth,
He sinned secure behind a veil of truth.
Some lock their lips upon their deeds; some write
A damning record and conceal from sight;
Some, with a lust of speaking, die to quell it.
His way to keep a secret was to tell it.

Stephen J. Field
Here sleeps one of the greatest students
Of jurisprudence.
Nature endowed him with the gift
Of the juristhrift.
All points of law alike he threw
The dice to settle.
Those honest cubes were loaded true
With railway metal.

Stoneman In Heaven

The Seraphs came to Christ, and said: 'Behold!
The man, presumptuous and overbold,
Who boasted that his mercy could excel
Thine own, is dead and on his way to Hell.'
Gravely the Saviour asked: 'What did he do
To make his impious assertion true?'
'He was a Governor, releasing all
The vilest felons ever held in thrall.
No other mortal, since the dawn of time,
Has ever pardoned such a mass of crime!'
Christ smiled benignly on the Seraphim:
'Yet I am victor, for I pardon him.'

Strained Relations

Says England to Germany: 'Africa's ours.'
Says Germany: 'Ours, I opine.'
Says Africa: 'Tell me, delectable Pow'rs,
What is it that ought to be mine?'

Substance Versus Shadow

So, gentle critics, you would have me tilt,
Not at the guilty, only just at Guilt!
Spare the offender and condemn Offense,
And make life miserable to Pretense!
'Whip Vice and Folly - that is satire's use
But be not personal, for that's abuse;
Nor e'er forget what, 'like a razor keen,
Wounds with a touch that's neither felt nor seen.''
Well, friends, I venture, destitute of awe,
To think that razor but an old, old saw,
A trifle rusty; and a wound, I'm sure,
That's felt not, seen not, one can well endure.
Go to! go to! you're as unfitted quite
To give advice to writers as to write.
I find in Folly and in Vice a lack
Of head to hit, and for the lash no back;
Whilst Pixley has a pow that's easy struck,
And though good Deacon Fitch (a Fitch for luck!)
Has none, yet, lest he go entirely free,
God gave to him a corn, a heel to me.
He, also, sets his face (so like a flint
The wonder grows that Pickering doesn't skin't)
With cold austerity, against these wars
On scamps - 'tis Scampery that he abhors!
Behold advance in dignity and state
Grave, smug, serene, indubitably great

Stanford, philanthropist! One hand bestows
In alms what t'other one as justice owes.
Rascality attends him like a shade,
But closes, woundless, o'er my baffled blade,
Its limbs unsevered, spirit undismayed.
Faith! I'm for something can be made to feel,
If, like Pelides, only in the heel.
The fellow's self invites assault; his crimes
Will each bear killing twenty thousand times!
Anon Creed Haymond - but the list is long
Of names to point the moral of my song.
Rogues, fools, impostors, sycophants, they rise,
They foul the earth and horrify the skies
With Mr. Huntington (sole honest man
In all the reek of that rapscallion clan)
Denouncing Theft as hard as e'er he can!

Subterranean Phantasies
I died. As meekly in the earth I lay,
With shriveled fingers reverently folded,
The worm uncivil engineer! my clay
Tunneled industriously, and the mole did.
My body could not dodge them, but my soul did;
For that had flown from this terrestrial ball
And I was rid of it for good and all.
So there I lay, debating what to do
What measures might most usefully be taken
To circumvent the subterranean crew
Of anthropophagi and save my bacon.
My fortitude was all this while unshaken,
But any gentleman, of course, protests
Against receiving uninvited guests.
However proud he might be of his meats,
Not even Apicius, nor, I think, Lucullus,
Wasted on tramps his culinary sweets;
'Aut Caesar,' say judicious hosts, 'aut nullus.'
And though when Marcius came unbidden Tullus
Aufidius feasted him because he starved,
Marcius by Tullus afterward was carved.
We feed the hungry, as the book commands
(For men might question else our orthodoxy)
But do not care to see the outstretched hands,
And so we minister to them by proxy.
When Want, in his improper person, knocks he
Finds we're engaged. The graveworm's very fresh
To think we like his presence in the flesh.
So, as I said, I lay in doubt; in all
That underworld no judges could determine
My rights. When Death approaches them they fall,

And falling, naturally soil their ermine.
And still below ground, as above, the vermin
That work by dark and silent methods win
The case - the burial case that one is in.
Cases at law so slowly get ahead,
Even when the right is visibly unclouded,
That if all men are classed as quick and dead,
The judges all are dead, though some unshrouded.
Pray Jove that when they're actually crowded
On Styx's brink, and Charon rows in sight,
His bark prove worse than Cerberus's bite.
Ah! Cerberus, if you had but begot
A race of three-mouthed dogs for man to nourish
And woman to caress, the muse had not
Lamented the decay of virtues currish,
And triple-hydrophobia now would flourish,
For barking, biting, kissing to employ
Canine repeaters were indeed a joy.
Lord! how we cling to this vile world! Here I,
Whose dust was laid ere I began this carping,
By moles and worms and such familiar fry
Run through and through, am singing still and harping
Of mundane matters-flatting, too, and sharping.
I hate the Angel of the Sleeping Cup:
So I'm for getting - and for shutting-up.

Surprised

'O son of mine age, these eyes lose their fire:
Be eyes, I pray, to thy dying sire.'
'O father, fear not, for mine eyes are bright
I read through a millstone at dead of night.'
'My son, O tell me, who are those men,
Rushing like pigs to the feeding-pen?'
'Welcomers they of a statesman grand.
They'll shake, and then they will pocket; his hand.'
'Sagacious youth, with the wondrous eye,
They seem to throw up their headgear. Why?'
'Because they've thrown up their hands until,
O, They're so tired! and dinners they've none to throw.'
'My son, my son, though dull are mine ears,
I hear a great sound like the people's cheers.'
'He's thanking them, father, with tears in his eyes,
For giving him lately that fine surprise.'
'My memory fails as I near mine end;
How did they astonish their grateful friend?'
'By letting him buy, like apples or oats,
With that which has made him so good, the votes
Which make him so wise and grand and great.
Now, father, please die, for 'tis growing late.'

T.A.H.

Yes, he was that, or that, as you prefer,
Did so and so, though, faith, it was n't all;
Lived like a fool, or a philosopher,
And had whatever's needful to a fall.
As rough inflections on a planet merge
In the true bend of the gigantic sphere,
Nor mar the perfect circle of its verge,
So in the survey of his worth the small
Asperities of spirit disappear,
Lost in the grander curves of character.
He lately was hit hard; none knew but I
The strength and terror of that ghastly stroke,
Not even herself. He uttered not a cry,
But set his teeth and made a revelry;
Drank like a devil,—staining sometimes red
The goblet 's edge; diced with his conscience; spread,
Like Sisyphus, a feast for Death, and spoke
His welcome in a tongue so long forgot
That even his ancient guest remembered not
What race had cursed him in it. Thus my friend,
Still conjugating with each failing sense
The verb "to die" in every mood and tense,
Pursued his awful humor to the end.
When, like a stormy dawn, the crimson broke
From his white lips, he smiled and mutely bled,
And, having meanly lived, is grandly dead.

Technology

'Twas a serious person with locks of gray
And a figure like a crescent;
His gravity, clearly, had come to stay,
But his smile was evanescent.
He stood and conversed with a neighbor, and
With (likewise) a high falsetto;
And he stabbed his forefinger into his hand
As if it had been a stiletto.
His words, like the notes of a tenor drum,
Came out of his head unblended,
And the wonderful altitude of some
Was exceptionally splendid.
While executing a shake of the head,
With the hand, as it were, of a master,
This agonizing old gentleman said:
"Twas a truly sad disaster!
'Four hundred and ten longs and shorts in all,

Went down' - he paused and snuffled.
A single tear was observed to fall,
And the old man's drum was muffled.
'A very calamitous year,' he said.
And again his head-piece hoary
He shook, and another pearl he shed,
As if he wept con amore.
'O lacrymose person,' I cried, 'pray why
Should these failures so affect you?
With speculators in stocks no eye
That's normal would ever connect you.'
He focused his orbs upon mine and smiled
In a sinister sort of manner.
'Young man,' he said, 'your words are wild:
I spoke of the steamship 'Hanner.'
'For she has went down in a howlin' squall,
And my heart is nigh to breakin'
Four hundred and ten longs and shorts in all
Will never need undertakin'!
'I'm in the business myself,' said he,
'And you've mistook my expression;
For I uses the technical terms, you see,
Employed in my perfession.'
That old undertaker has joined the throng
On the other side of the River,
But I'm still unhappy to think I'm a 'long,'
And a tape-line makes me shiver.

Tempora Mutantur
'The world is dull,' I cried in my despair:
'Its myths and fables are no longer fair.
'Roll back thy centuries, O Father Time.
To Greece transport me in her golden prime.
'Give back the beautiful old Gods again
The sportive Nymphs, the Dryad's jocund train,
'Pan piping on his reeds, the Naiades,
The Sirens singing by the sleepy seas.
'Nay, show me but a Gorgon and I'll dare
To lift mine eyes to her peculiar hair
'(The fatal horrors of her snaky pate,
That stiffen men into a stony state)
'And die-erecting, as my soul goes hence,
A statue of myself, without expense.'
Straight as I spoke I heard the voice of Fate:
'Look up, my lad, the Gorgon sisters wait.'
Raising my eyes, I saw Medusa stand,
Stheno, Euryale, on either hand.
I gazed unpetrified and unappalled
The girls had aged and were entirely bald!

The Aesthetes

The lily cranks, the lily cranks,
The loppy, loony lasses!
They multiply in rising ranks
To execute their solemn pranks,
They moon along in masses.
Blow, sweet lily, in the shade! O,
Sunflower decorate the dado!
The maiden ass, the maiden ass,
The tall and tailless jenny!
In limp attire as green as grass,
She stands, a monumental brass,
The one of one too many.
Blow, sweet lily, in the shade! O,
Sunflower decorate the dado!

The American Party

Oh, Marcus D. Boruck, me hearty,
I sympathize wid ye, poor lad!
A man that's shot out of his party
Is mighty onlucky, bedad!
An' the sowl o' that man is sad.
But, Marcus, gossoon, ye desarve it
Ye know for yerself that ye do,
For ye j'ined not intendin' to sarve it,
But hopin' to make it sarve you,
Though the roll of its members wuz two.
The other wuz Pixley, an' 'Surely,'
Ye said, 'he's a kite that wall sail.'
An' so ye hung till him securely,
Enactin' the role of a tail.
But there wuzn't the ghost of a gale!
But the party to-day has behind it
A powerful backin', I'm told;
For just enough Irish have j'ined it
(An' I'm m'anin' to be enrolled)
To kick ye out into the cold.
It's hard on ye, darlint, I'm thinkin'
So young - so American, too
Wid bypassers grinnin' an' winkin',
An' sayin', wid ref'rence to you:
'Get onto the murtherin' Joo!'
Republicans never will take ye
They had ye for many a year;
An' Dimocrats angels forsake ye!
If ever ye come about here

We'll brand ye and scollop yer ear!

The Barking Weasel

You say, John Irish, Mr. Taylor hath
A painted beard. Quite likely that is true,
And sure 'tis natural you spend your wrath
On what has been least merciful to you.
By Taylor's chin, if I am not mistaken,
You like a rat have recently been shaken.
To wear a beard of artificial hue
May be or this or that, I know not what;
But, faith, 'tis better to be black and blue
In beard from dallying with brush and pot
Than to be so in body from the beating
That hardy rogues get when detected cheating.
You're whacked about the mazzard rather more
Of late than any other man in town.
Certes your vulnerable back is sore
And tender, too, your corrigible crown.
In truth your whole periphery discloses
More vivid colors than a bed of posies!
You call it glory! Put your tongue in sheath!
Scars got in battle, even if on the breast,
May be a shameful record if, beneath,
A robber heart a lawless strife attest.
John Sullivan had wounds, and Paddy Ryan
Nay, as to that, even Masten has, and Bryan.
'Tis willingly conceded you've a knack
At holding the attention of the town;
The worse for you when you have on your back
What did not grow there - prithee put it down!
For pride kills thrift, and you lack board and lodging,
Even while the brickbats of renown you're dodging.

The Birth Of Virtue

When, long ago, the young world circling flew
Through wider reaches of a richer blue,
New-eyed, the men and maids saw, manifest,
The thoughts untold in one another's breast:
Each wish displayed, and every passion learned
A look revealed them as a look discerned.
But sating Time with clouds o'ercast their eyes;
Desire was hidden, and the lips framed lies.
A goddess then, emerging from the dust,
Fair Virtue rose, the daughter of Distrust.

The Boss's Choice
Listen to his wild romances:
He advances foolish fancies,
Each expounded as his 'view'
Gu.
In his brain's opacous clot, ah
He has got a maggot! What a
Man with 'views' to overwhelm us!
Gulielmus.
Hear his demagogic clamor
Hear him stammer in his grammar!
Teaching, he will learn to spell
Gulielmus L.
Slave who paid the price demanded
With two-handed iron branded
By the boss pray cease to dose us,
Gulielmus L. Jocosus.

The Bride
"You know, my friends, with what a brave carouse
I made a second marriage in my house,—
Divorced old barren Reason from my bed
And took the Daughter of the Vine to spouse."
So sang the Lord of Poets. In a gleam
Of light that made her like an angel seem,
The Daughter of the Vine said: "I myself
Am Reason, and the Other was a Dream."

The Committee On Public Morals
The Senate met in Sacramento city;
On public morals it had no committee
Though greatly these abounded. Soon the quiet
Was broken by the Senators in riot.
Now, at the end of their contagious quarrels,
There's a committee but no public morals.

The Confederate Flags
Tut-tut! give back the flags - how can you care,
You veterans and heroes?
Why should you at a kind intention swear
Like twenty Neros?
Suppose the act was not so overwise
Suppose it was illegal;
Is't well on such a question to arise

And punch the Eagle?
Nay, let's economize his breath to scold
And terrify the alien
Who tackles him, as Hercules of old
The bird Stymphalian.
Among the rebels when we made a breach
Was it to get the banners?
That was but incidental - 'twas to teach
Them better manners.
They know the lessons well enough to-day;
Now, let us try to show them
That we're not only stronger far than they,
(How we did mow them!)
But more magnanimous. My lads, 'tis plain
'Twas an uncommon riot;
The warlike tribes of Europe fight for gain;
We fought for quiet.
If we were victors, then we all must live
With the same flag above us;
'Twas all in vain unless we now forgive
And make them love us.
Let kings keep trophies to display above
Their doors like any savage;
The freeman's trophy is the foeman's love,
Despite war's ravage.
'Make treason odious?' My friends, you'll find
You can't, in right and reason,
While 'Washington' and 'treason' are combined
'Hugo' and 'treason.'
All human governments must take the chance
And hazard of sedition.
O wretch! to pledge your manhood in advance
To blind submission.
It may be wrong, it may be right, to rise
In warlike insurrection:
The loyalty that fools so dearly prize
May mean subjection.
Be loyal to your country, yes - but how
If tyrants hold dominion?
The South believed they did; can't you allow
For that opinion?
He who will never rise though rulers plot,
His liberties despising
He is he manlier than the sans-culottes
Who's always rising?
Give back the foolish flags whose bearers fell,
Too valiant to forsake them.
Is it presumptuous, this counsel? Well,
I helped to take them.

The Convicts' Ball
San Quentin was brilliant. Within the halls
Of the noble pile with the frowning walls
(God knows they've enough to make them frown,
With a Governor trying to break them down!)
Was a blaze of light. 'Twas the natal day
Of his nibs the popular John S. Gray,
And many observers considered his birth
The primary cause of his moral worth.
'The ball is free!' cried Black Bart, and they all
Said a ball with no chain was a novel ball;
'And I never have seed,' said Jimmy Hope,
'Sech a lightsome dance withouten a rope.'
Chinamen, Indians, Portuguese, Blacks,
Russians, Italians, Kanucks and Kanaks,
Chilenos, Peruvians, Mexicans all
Greased with their presence that notable ball.
None were excluded excepting, perhaps,
The Rev. Morrison's churchly chaps,
Whom, to prevent a religious debate,
The Warden had banished outside of the gate.
The fiddler, fiddling his hardest the while,
'Called off' in the regular foot-hill style:
'Circle to the left!' and 'Forward and back!'
And 'Hellum to port for the stabbard tack!'
(This great virtuoso, it would appear,
Was Mate of the Gatherer many a year.)
'Ally man left!' to a painful degree
His French was unlike to the French of Paree,
As heard from our countrymen lately abroad,
And his 'doe cee doe' was the gem of the fraud.
But what can you hope from a gentleman barred
From circles of culture by dogs in the yard?
'Twas a glorious dance, though, all the same,
The Jardin Mabille in the days of its fame
Never saw legs perform such springs
The cold-chisel's magic had given them wings.
They footed it featly, those lades and gents:
Dull care (said Long Moll) had a helly go-hence!
'Twas a very aristocratic affair:
The creme de la creme and elite were there
Rank, beauty and wealth from the highest sets,
And Hubert Howe Bancroft sent his regrets.

The Cynic's Bequest
In that fair city, Ispahan,
There dwelt a problematic man,
Whose angel never was released,

Who never once let out his beast,
But kept, through all the seasons' round,
Silence unbroken and profound.
No Prophecy, with ear applied
To key-hole of the future, tried
Successfully to catch a hint
Of what he'd do nor when begin 't;
As sternly did his past defy
Mild Retrospection's backward eye.
Though all admired his silent ways,
The women loudest were in praise:
For ladies love those men the most
Who never, never, never boast
Who ne'er disclose their aims and ends
To naughty, naughty, naughty friends.
Yet, sooth to say, the fame outran
The merit of this doubtful man,
For taciturnity in him,
Though not a mere caprice or whim,
Was not a virtue, such as truth,
High birth, or beauty, wealth or youth.
'Twas known, indeed, throughout the span
Of Ispahan, of Gulistan
These utmost limits of the earth
Knew that the man was dumb from birth.
Unto the Sun with deep salaams
The Parsee spreads his morning palms
(A beacon blazing on a height
Warms o'er his piety by night.)
The Moslem deprecates the deed,
Cuts off the head that holds the creed,
Then reverently goes to grass,
Muttering thanks to Balaam's Ass
For faith and learning to refute
Idolatry so dissolute!
But should a maniac dash past,
With straws in beard and hands upcast,
To him (through whom, whene'er inclined
To preach a bit to Madmankind,
The Holy Prophet speaks his mind)
Our True Believer lifts his eyes
Devoutly and his prayer applies;
But next to Solyman the Great
Reveres the idiot's sacred state.
Small wonder then, our worthy mute
Was held in popular repute.
Had he been blind as well as mum,
Been lame as well as blind and dumb,
No bard that ever sang or soared
Could say how he had been adored.
More meagerly endowed, he drew

An homage less prodigious. True,
No soul his praises but did utter
All plied him with devotion's butter,
But none had out - 't was to their credit
The proselyting sword to spread it.
I state these truths, exactly why
The reader knows as well as I;
They've nothing in the world to do
With what I hope we're coming to
If Pegasus be good enough
To move when he has stood enough.
Egad! his ribs I would examine
Had I a sharper spur than famine,
Or even with that if 'twould incline
To examine his instead of mine.
Where was I? Ah, that silent man
Who dwelt one time in Ispahan
He had a name - was known to all
As Meerza Solyman Zingall.
There lived afar in Astrabad,
A man the world agreed was mad,
So wickedly he broke his joke
Upon the heads of duller folk,
So miserly, from day to day,
He gathered up and hid away
In vaults obscure and cellars haunted
What many worthy people wanted,
A stingy man! the tradesmen's palms
Were spread in vain: 'I give no alms
Without inquiry' - so he'd say,
And beat the needy duns away.
The bastinado did, 'tis true,
Persuade him, now and then, a few
Odd tens of thousands to disburse
To glut the taxman's hungry purse,
But still, so rich he grew, his fear
Was constant that the Shah might hear.
(The Shah had heard it long ago,
And asked the taxman if 'twere so,
Who promptly answered, rather airish,
The man had long been on the parish.)
The more he feared, the more he grew
A cynic and a miser, too,
Until his bitterness and pelf
Made him a terror to himself;
Then, with a razor's neckwise stroke,
He tartly cut his final joke.
So perished, not an hour too soon,
The wicked Muley Ben Maroon.
From Astrabad to Ispahan
At camel speed the rumor ran

That, breaking through tradition hoar,
And throwing all his kinsmen o'er,
The miser'd left his mighty store
Of gold - his palaces and lands
To needy and deserving hands
(Except a penny here and there
To pay the dervishes for prayer.)
'Twas known indeed throughout the span
Of earth, and into Hindostan,
That our beloved mute was the
Residuary legatee.
The people said 'twas very well,
And each man had a tale to tell
Of how he'd had a finger in 't
By dropping many a friendly hint
At Astrabad, you see. But ah,
They feared the news might reach the Shah!
To prove the will the lawyers bore 't
Before the Kadi's awful court,
Who nodded, when he heard it read,
Confirmingly his drowsy head,
Nor thought, his sleepiness so great,
Himself to gobble the estate.
'I give,' the dead had writ, 'my all
To Meerza Solyman Zingall
Of Ispahan. With this estate
I might quite easily create
Ten thousand ingrates, but I shun
Temptation and create but one,
In whom the whole unthankful crew
The rich man's air that ever drew
To fat their pauper lungs I fire
Vicarious with vain desire!
From foul Ingratitude's base rout
I pick this hapless devil out,
Bestowing on him all my lands,
My treasures, camels, slaves and bands
Of wives - I give him all this loot,
And throw my blessing in to boot.
Behold, O man, in this bequest
Philanthropy's long wrongs redressed:
To speak me ill that man I dower
With fiercest will who lacks the power.
Allah il Allah! now let him bloat
With rancor till his heart's afloat,
Unable to discharge the wave
Upon his benefactor's grave!'
Forth in their wrath the people came
And swore it was a sin and shame
To trick their blessed mute; and each
Protested, serious of speech,

That though he'd long foreseen the worst
He'd been against it from the first.
By various means they vainly tried
The testament to set aside,
Each ready with his empty purse
To take upon himself the curse;
For they had powers of invective
Enough to make it ineffective.
The ingrates mustered, every man,
And marched in force to Ispahan
(Which had not quite accommodation)
And held a camp of indignation.
The man, this while, who never spoke
On whom had fallen this thunder-stroke
Of fortune, gave no feeling vent
Nor dropped a clue to his intent.
Whereas no power to him came
His benefactor to defame,
Some (such a length had slander gone to)
Even whispered that he didn't want to!
But none his secret could divine;
If suffering he made no sign,
Until one night as winter neared
From all his haunts he disappeared
Evanished in a doubtful blank
Like little crayfish in a bank,
Their heads retracting for a spell,
And pulling in their holes as well.
All through the land of Gul, the stout
Young Spring is kicking Winter out.
The grass sneaks in upon the scene,
Defacing it with bottle-green.
The stumbling lamb arrives to ply
His restless tail in every eye,
Eats nasty mint to spoil his meat
And make himself unfit to eat.
Madly his throat the bulbul tears
In every grove blasphemes and swears
As the immodest rose displays
Her shameless charms a dozen ways.
Lo! now, throughout the utmost span
Of Ispahan - of Gulistan
A big new book's displayed in all
The shops and cumbers every stall.
The price is low - the dealers say 'tis
And the rich are treated to it gratis.
Engraven on its foremost page
These title words the eye engage:
'The Life of Muley Ben Maroon,
Of Astrabad, Rogue, Thief, Buffoon
And Miser-Liver by the Sweat

Of Better Men: A Lamponette
Composed in Rhyme and Written all
By Meerza Solyman Zingall!'

The Day Of Wrath / Dies Iræ
Day of Satan's painful duty!   Dies iræ! dies illa!
Earth shall vanish, hot and sooty;   Solvet sæclum in favilla
So says Virtue, so says Beauty.   Teste David cum Sibylla.
Ah! what terror shall be shaping   Quantus tremor est futurus,
When the Judge the truth's undraping   Quando Judex est venturus.
Cats from every bag escaping!   Cuncta stricte discussurus.
Now the trumpet's invocation   Tuba mirum spargens sonum
Calls the dead to condemnation;   Per sepulchra regionem,
All receive an invitation.   Coget omnes ante thronum
Death and Nature now are quaking,   Mors stupebit, et Natura,
And the late lamented, waking,   Quum resurget creatura
In their breezy shrouds are shaking.   Judicanti responsura.
Lo! the Ledger's leaves are stirring,   Liber scriptus proferetur,
And the Clerk, to them referring,   In quo totum continetur,
Makes it awkward for the erring.   Unde mundus judicetur.
When the Judge appears in session,   Judex ergo quum sedebit,
We shall all attend confession,   Quicquid latet apparebit,
Loudly preaching non-suppression.   Nil inultum remanebit.
How shall I then make romances   Quid sum miser tunc dicturus,
Mitigating circumstances?   Quem patronem rogaturus,
Even the just must take their chances.   Quum vix justus sit securus?
King whose majesty amazes,   Rex tremendæ majestatis,
Save thou him who sings thy praises;   Qui salvandos salvas gratis;
Fountain, quench my private blazes.   Salva me, Fons pietatis.
Pray remember, sacred Saviour,   Recordare, Jesu pie,
Mine the playful hand that gave your   Quod sum causa tuæ viæ;
Death-blow. Pardon such behavior.   Ne me perdas illa die.
Seeking me, fatigue assailed thee,   Quærens me sedisti lassus
Calvary's outlook naught availed thee;   Redemisti crucem passus,
Now 'twere cruel if I failed thee.   Tantus labor non sit cassus.
Righteous judge and learnèd brother,   Juste Judex ultionis,
Pray thy prejudices smother   Donum fac remissionis
Ere we meet to try each other.   Ante diem rationis.
Sighs of guilt my conscience gushes,   Ingemisco tanquam reus,
And my face vermilion flushes;   Culpa rubet vultus meus;
Spare me for my pretty blushes.   Supplicanti parce, Deus.
Thief and harlot, when repenting,   Qui Mariam absolvisti,
Thou forgavest - complimenting   Et latronem exaudisti,
Me with sign of like relenting.   Mihi quoque spem dedisti.
If too bold is my petition   Preces meæ non sunt dignæ,
I'll receive with due submission   Sed to bonus fac benigne
My dismissal from perdition.   Ne perenni cremer igne.
When thy sheep thou hast selected   Inter oves locum præsta.
From the goats, may I, respected,   Et ab hædis me sequestra,

Stand amongst them undetected.   Statuens in parte dextra.
When offenders are indited,   Confutatis maledictis,
And with trial flames ignited,   Flammis acribus addictis,
Elsewhere I'll attend if cited.   Voca me cum benedictis.
Ashen hearted, prone and prayerful,   Oro supplex et acclinis,
When of death I see the air full,   Cor contritum quasi cinis;
Lest I perish too be careful.   Gere curam mei finis.
On that day of lamentation,   Lacrymosa dies illa
When, to enjoy the conflagration,   Qua resurget et favilla,
Men come forth, O be not cruel: Judicandus homo reus, Spare me,
Lord - make them thy fuel.   Huic ergo parce, Deus!

The Dead King

Hawaii's King resigned his breath
Our Legislature guffawed.
The awful dignity of death
Not any single rough awed.
But when our Legislators die
All Kings, Queens, Jacks and Aces cry.

The Death Of Grant

Father! whose hard and cruel law
Is part of thy compassion's plan,
Thy works presumptuously we scan
For what the prophets say they saw.
Unbidden still the awful slope
Walling us in we climb to gain
Assurance of the shining plain
That faith has certified to hope.
In vain! - beyond the circling hill
The shadow and the cloud abide.
Subdue the doubt, our spirits guide
To trust the record and be still.
To trust it loyally as he
Who, heedful of his high design,
Ne'er raised a seeking eye to thine,
But wrought thy will unconsciously.
Disputing not of chance or fate,
Nor questioning of cause or creed:
For anything but duty's deed
Too simply wise, too humbly grave.
The cannon syllabled his name;
His shadow shifted o'er the land,
Portentous, as at his demand
Successive battalions sprang to flame!
He flared the continent with fire,
The rivers ran in lines of light!

Thy will be done on earth - if right
Or wrong he cared not to inquire.
His was the heavy hand, and his
The service of the despot blade;
His the soft answer that allayed
War's giant animosities.
Let us have peace: our clouded eyes,
Fill, Father, with another light,
That we may see with clearer sight
Thy servant's soul in Paradise.

The Debtor Abroad
Grief for an absent lover, husband, friend,
Is barely felt before it comes to end:
A score of early consolations serve
To modify its mouth's dejected curve.
But woes of creditors when debtors flee
Forever swell the separating sea.
When standing on an alien shore you mark
The steady course of some intrepid bark,
How sweet to think a tear for you abides,
Not all unuseful, in the wave she rides!
That sighs for you commingle in the gale
Beneficently bellying her sail!

The Division Superintendent
Baffled he stands upon the track
The automatic switches clack.
Where'er he turns his solemn eyes
The interlocking signals rise.
The trains, before his visage pale,
Glide smoothly by, nor leave the rail.
No splinter-spitted victim he
Hears uttering the note high C.
In sorrow deep he hangs his head,
A-weary would that he were dead.
Now suddenly his spirits rise
A great thought kindles in his eyes.
Hope, like a headlight's vivid glare,
Splendors the path of his despair.
His genius shines, the clouds roll back
'I'll place obstructions on the track!'

The Dying Statesman
It is a politician man

He draweth near his end,
And friends weep round that partisan,
Of every man the friend.
Between the Known and the Unknown
He lieth on the strand;
The light upon the sea is thrown
That lay upon the land.
It shineth in his glazing eye,
It burneth on his face;
God send that when we come to die
We know that sign of grace!
Upon his lips his blessed sprite
Poiseth her joyous wing.
'How is it with thee, child of light?
Dost hear the angels sing?'
'The song I hear, the crown I see,
And know that God is love.
Farewell, dark world - I go to be
A postmaster above!'
For him no monumental arch,
But, O, 'tis good and brave
To see the Grand Old Party march
To office o'er his grave!

The Eastern Question

Looking across the line, the Grecian said:
'This border I will stain a Turkey red.'
The Moslem smiled securely and replied:
'No Greek has ever for his country dyed.'
While thus each patriot guarded his frontier,
The Powers stole all the country in his rear.

The Fall Of Miss Larkin

Hear me sing of Sally Larkin who, I'd have you understand,
Played accordions as well as any lady in the land;
And I've often heard it stated that her fingering was such
That Professor Schweinenhauer was enchanted with her touch;
And that beasts were so affected when her apparatus rang
That they dropped upon their haunches and deliriously sang.
This I know from testimony, though a critic, I opine,
Needs an ear that is dissimilar in some respects to mine.
She could sing, too, like a jaybird, and they say all eyes were wet
When Sally and the ranch-dog were performing a duet
Which I take it is a song that has to be so loudly sung
As to overtax the strength of any single human lung.
That, at least, would seem to follow from the tale I have to tell,
Which (I've told you how she flourished) is how Sally Larkin fell.

One day there came to visit Sally's dad as sleek and smart
A chap as ever wandered there from any foreign part.
Though his gentle birth and breeding he did not at all obtrude
It was somehow whispered round he was a simon pure Dude.
Howsoe'er that may have been, it was conspicuous to see
That he was a real Gent of an uncommon high degree.
That Sally cast her tender and affectionate regards
On this exquisite creation was, of course, upon the cards;
But he didn't seem to notice, and was variously blind
To her many charms of person and the merits of her mind,
And preferred, I grieve to say it, to play poker with her dad,
And acted in a manner that in general was bad.
One evening 'twas in summer - she was holding in her lap
Her accordion, and near her stood that melancholy chap,
Leaning up against a pillar with his lip in grog imbrued,
Thinking, maybe, of that ancient land in which he was a Dude.
Then Sally, who was melancholy too, began to hum
And elongate the accordion with a preluding thumb.
Then sighs of amorosity from Sally L. exhaled,
And her music apparatus sympathetically wailed.
'In the gloaming, O my darling!' rose that wild impassioned strain,
And her eyes were fixed on his with an intensity of pain,
Till the ranch-dog from his kennel at the postern gate came round,
And going into session strove to magnify the sound.
He lifted up his spirit till the gloaming rang and rang
With the song that to his darling he impetuously sang!
Then that musing youth, recalling all his soul from other scenes,
Where his fathers all were Dudes and his mothers all Dudines,
From his lips removed the beaker and politely, o'er the grog,
Said: 'Miss Larkin, please be quiet: you will interrupt the dog.'

The Following Pair

O very remarkable mortal,
What food is engaging your jaws
And staining with amber their portal?
'It's 'baccy I chaws.'
And why do you sway in your walking,
To right and left many degrees,
And hitch up your trousers when talking?
'I follers the seas.'
Great indolent shark in the rollers,
Is "baccy,' too, one of your faults?
You, too, display maculate molars.
'I dines upon salts.'
Strange diet! intestinal pain it
Is commonly given to nip.
And how can you ever obtain it?
'I follers the ship.'

The Foot-Hill Resort
Assembled in the parlor
Of the place of last resort,
The smiler and the snarler
And the guests of every sort
The elocution chap
With rhetoric on tap;
The mimic and the funny dog;
The social sponge; the money-hog;
Vulgarian and dude;
And the prude;
The adiposing dame
With pimply face aflame;
The kitten-playful virgin
Vergin' on to fifty years;
The solemn looking sturgeon
Of a firm of auctioneers;
The widower flirtatious;
The widow all too gracious;
The man with a proboscis and a sepulcher beneath.
One assassin picks the banjo, and another picks his teeth.

The Fountain Refilled
Of Hans Pietro Shanahan
(Who was a most ingenious man)
The Muse of History records
That he'd get drunk as twenty lords.
He'd get so truly drunk that men
Stood by to marvel at him when
His slow advance along the street
Was but a vain cycloidal feat.
And when 'twas fated that he fall
With a wide geographical sprawl,
They signified assent by sounds
Heard (faintly) at its utmost bounds.
And yet this Mr. Shanahan
(Who was a most ingenious man)
Cast not on wine his thirsty eyes
When it was red or otherwise.
All malt, or spirituous, tope
He loathed as cats dissent from soap;
And cider, if it touched his lip,
Evoked a groan at every sip.
But still, as heretofore explained,
He not infrequently was grained.
(I'm not of those who call it 'corned.'
Coarse speech I've always duly scorned.)

Though truth to say, and that's but right,
Strong drink (it hath an adder's bite!)
Was what had put him in the mud,
The only kind he used was blood!
Alas, that an immortal soul
Addicted to the flowing bowl,
The emptied flagon should again
Replenish from a neighbor's vein.
But, Mr. Shanahan was so
Constructed, and his taste that low.
Nor more deplorable was he
In kind of thirst than in degree;
For sometimes fifty souls would pay
The debt of nature in a day
To free him from the shame and pain
Of dread Sobriety's misreign.
His native land, proud of its sense
Of his unique inabstinence,
Abated something of its pride
At thought of his unfilled inside.
And some the boldness had to say
'Twere well if he were called away
To slake his thirst forevermore
In oceans of celestial gore.
But Hans Pietro Shanahan
(Who was a most ingenious man)
Knew that his thirst was mortal; so
Remained unsainted here below
Unsainted and unsaintly, for
He neither went to glory nor
To abdicate his power deigned
Where, under Providence, he reigned,
But kept his Boss's power accurst
To serve his wild uncommon thirst.
Which now had grown so truly great
It was a drain upon the State.
Soon, soon there came a time, alas!
When he turned down an empty glass
All practicable means were vain
His special wassail to obtain.
In vain poor Decimation tried
To furnish forth the needful tide;
And Civil War as vainly shed
Her niggard offering of red.
Poor Shanahan! his thirst increased
Until he wished himself deceased,
Invoked the firearm and the knife,
But could not die to save his life!
He was so dry his own veins made
No answer to the seeking blade;
So parched that when he would have passed

Away he could not breathe his last.
'Twas then, when almost in despair,
(Unlaced his shoon, unkempt his hair)
He saw as in a dream a way
To wet afresh his mortal clay.
Yes, Hans Pietro Shanahan
(Who was a most ingenious man)
Saw freedom, and with joy and pride
'Thalassa! (or Thalatta!)' cried.
Straight to the Aldermen went he,
With many a 'pull' and many a fee,
And many a most corrupt 'combine'
(The Press for twenty cents a line
Held out and fought him - O, God, bless
Forevermore the holy Press!)
Till he had franchises complete
For trolley lines on every street!
The cars were builded and, they say,
Were run on rails laid every way
Rhomboidal roads, and circular,
And oval everywhere a car
Square, dodecagonal (in great
Esteem the shape called Figure 8)
And many other kinds of shapes
As various as tails of apes.
No other group of men's abodes
E'er had such odd electric roads,
That winding in and winding out,
Began and ended all about.
No city had, unless in Mars,
That city's wealth of trolley cars.
They ran by day, they flew by night,
And O, the sorry, sorry sight!
And Hans Pietro Shanahan
(Who was a most ingenious man)
Incessantly, the Muse records,
Lay drunk as twenty thousand lords!

The Free Trader's Lament

Oft from a trading-boat I purchased spice
And shells and corals, brought for my inspection
From the fair tropics - paid a Christian price
And was content in my fool's paradise,
Where never had been heard the word 'Protection.'
'T was my sole island; there I dwelt alone
No customs house, collector nor collection,
But a man came, who, In a pious tone
Condoled with me that I had never known
The manifest advantage of Protection.

So, when the trading-boat arrived one day,
He threw a stink-pot into its mid-section.
The traders paddled for their lives away,
Nor came again into that haunted bay,
The blessed home thereafter of Protection.
Then down he sat, that philanthropic man,
And spat upon some mud of his selection,
And worked it, with his knuckles in a pan,
To shapes of shells and coral things, and span
A thread of song in glory of Protection.
He baked them in the sun. His air devout
Enchanted me. I made a genuflexion:
'God help you, gentle sir,' I said. 'No doubt,'
He answered gravely, 'I'll get on without
Assistance now that we have got Protection.'
Thenceforth I bought his wares - at what a price
For shells and corals of such imperfection!
'Ah, now,' said he, 'your lot is truly nice.'
But still in all that isle there was no spice
To season to my taste that dish, Protection.

The Fyghtynge Seventh

It is the gallant Seventh
It fyghteth faste and free!
God wot the where it fyghteth
I ne desyre to be.
The Gonfalon it flyeth,
Seeming a Flayme in Sky;
The Bugel loud yblowen is,
Which sayeth, Doe and dye!
And (O good Saints defende us
Agaynst the Woes of Warr)
Drawn Tongues are flashing deadly
To smyte the Foeman sore!
With divers kinds of Riddance
The smoking Earth is wet,
And all aflowe to seaward goe
The Torrents wide of Sweat!
The Thunder of the Captens,
And eke the Shouting, mayketh
Such horrid Din the Soule within
The boddy of me quayketh!
Who fyghteth the bold Seventh?
What haughty Power defyes?
Their Colonel 'tis they drubben sore,
And dammen too his Eyes!

The Gates Ajar

The Day of Judgment spread its glare
O'er continents and seas.
The graves cracked open everywhere,
Like pods of early peas.
Up to the Court of Heaven sped
The souls of all mankind;
Republicans were at the head
And Democrats behind.
Reub. Lloyd was there before the tube
Of Gabriel could call:
The dead in Christ rise first, and Reub.
Had risen first of all.
He sat beside the Throne of Flame
As, to the trumpet's sound,
Four statesmen of the Party Came
And ranged themselves around
Pure spirits shining like the sun,
From taint and blemish free
Great William Stow was there for one,
And George A. Knight for three.
Souls less indubitably white
Approached with anxious air,
Judge Blake at head of them by right
Of having been a Mayor.
His ermine he had donned again,
Long laid away in gums.
'Twas soiled a trifle by the stains
Of politicians' thumbs.
Then Knight addressed the Judge of Heaven:
'Your Honor, would it trench
On custom here if Blake were given
A seat upon the Bench?'
'Twas done. 'Tom Shannon!' Peter cried.
He came, without ado,
In forma pauperis was tried,
And was acquitted, too!
Stow rose, remarking: 'I concur.'
Lloyd added: 'That suits us.
I move Tom's nomination, sir,
Be made unanimous.'

The Genesis Of Embarrassment

When Adam first saw Eve he said:
'O lovely creature, share my bed.'
Before consenting, she her gaze
Fixed on the greensward to appraise,
As well as vision could avouch,
The value of the proffered couch.

And seeing that the grass was green
And neatly clipped with a machine
Observing that the flow'rs were rare
Varieties, and some were fair,
The posts of precious woods, besprent
With fragrant balsams, diffluent,
And all things suited to her worth,
She raised her angel eyes from earth
To his and, blushing to confess,
Murmured: 'I love you, Adam - yes.'
Since then her daughters, it is said,
Look always down when asked to wed.

The God's View-Point

Cheeta Raibama Chunder Sen,
The wisest and the best of men,
Betook him to the place where sat
With folded feet upon a mat
Of precious stones beneath a palm,
In sweet and everlasting calm,
That ancient and immortal gent,
The God of Rational Content.
As tranquil and unmoved as Fate,
The deity reposed in state,
With palm to palm and sole to sole,
And beaded breast and beetling jowl,
And belly spread upon his thighs,
And costly diamonds for eyes.
As Chunder Sen approached and knelt
To show the reverence he felt;
Then beat his head upon the sod
To prove his fealty to the god;
And then by gestures signified
The other sentiments inside;
The god's right eye (as Chunder Sen,
The wisest and the best of men,
Half-fancied) grew by just a thought
More narrow than it truly ought.
Yet still that prince of devotees,
Persistent upon bended knees
And elbows bored into the earth,
Declared the god's exceeding worth,
And begged his favor. Then at last,
Within that cavernous and vast
Thoracic space was heard a sound
Like that of water underground
A gurgling note that found a vent
At mouth of that Immortal Gent
In such a chuckle as no ear

Had e'er been privileged to hear!
Cheeta Raibama Chunder Sen,
The wisest, greatest, best of men,
Heard with a natural surprise
That mighty midriff improvise.
And greater yet the marvel was
When from between those massive jaws
Fell words to make the views more plain
The god was pleased to entertain:
'Cheeta Raibama Chunder Sen,'
So ran the rede in speech of men
'Foremost of mortals in assent
To creed of Rational Content,
Why come you here to impetrate
A blessing on your scurvy pate?
Can you not rationally be
Content without disturbing me?
Can you not take a hint - a wink
Of what of all this rot I think?
Is laughter lost upon you quite,
To check you in your pious rite?
What! know you not we gods protest
That all religion is a jest?
You take me seriously? you
About me make a great ado
(When I but wish to be alone)
With attitudes supine and prone,
With genuflexions and with prayers,
And putting on of solemn airs,
To draw my mind from the survey
Of Rational Content away!
Learn once for all, if learn you can,
This truth, significant to man:
A pious person is by odds
The one most hateful to the gods.'
Then stretching forth his great right hand,
Which shadowed all that sunny land,
That deity bestowed a touch
Which Chunder Sen not overmuch
Enjoyed - a touch divine that made
The sufferer hear stars! They played
And sang as on Creation's morn
When spheric harmony was born.
Cheeta Raibama Chunder Sen,
The most astonished man of men,
Fell straight asleep, and when he woke
The deity nor moved nor spoke,
But sat beneath that ancient palm
In sweet and everlasting calm.

The Hermit

To a hunter from the city,
Overtaken by the night,
Spake, in tones of tender pity
For himself, an aged wight:
'I have found the world a fountain
Of deceit and Life a sham.
I have taken to the mountain
And a Holy Hermit am.
'Sternly bent on Contemplation,
Far apart from human kind
In the hill my habitation,
In the Infinite my mind.
'Ten long years I've lived a dumb thing,
Growing bald and bent with dole.
Vainly seeking for a Something
To engage my gloomy soul.
'Gentle Pilgrim, while my roots you
Eat, and quaff my simple drink,
Please suggest whatever suits you
As a Theme for me to Think.'
Then the hunter answered gravely:
'From distraction free, and strife,
You could ponder very bravely
On the Vanity of Life.'
'O, thou wise and learned Teacher,
You have solved the Problem well
You have saved a grateful creature
From the agonies of hell.
'Take another root, another
Cup of water: eat and drink.
Now I have a Subject, brother,
Tell me What, and How, to think.'

The Hesitating Veteran

When I was young and full of faith
And other fads that youngsters cherish
A cry rose as of one that saith
With emphasis: 'Help or I perish!'
'Twas heard in all the land, and men
The sound were each to each repeating.
It made my heart beat faster then
Than any heart can now be beating.
For the world is old and the world is gray
Grown prudent and, I think, more witty.
She's cut her wisdom teeth, they say,
And doesn't now go in for Pity.
Besides, the melancholy cry

Was that of one, 'tis now conceded,
Whose plight no one beneath the sky
Felt half so poignantly as he did.
Moreover, he was black. And yet
That sentimental generation
With an austere compassion set
Its face and faith to the occasion.
Then there were hate and strife to spare,
And various hard knocks a-plenty;
And I ('twas more than my true share,
I must confess) took five and twenty.
That all is over now - the reign
Of love and trade stills all dissensions,
And the clear heavens arch again
Above a land of peace and pensions.
The black chap - at the last we gave
Him everything that he had cried for,
Though many white chaps in the grave
'Twould puzzle to say what they died for.
I hope he's better off - I trust
That his society and his master's
Are worth the price we paid, and must
Continue paying, in disasters;
But sometimes doubts press thronging round
('Tis mostly when my hurts are aching)
If war for Union was a sound
And profitable undertaking.
'Tis said they mean to take away
The Negro's vote for he's unlettered.
'Tis true he sits in darkness day
And night, as formerly, when fettered;
But pray observe - howe'er he vote
To whatsoever party turning,
He'll be with gentlemen of note
And wealth and consequence and learning.
With saints and sages on each side,
How could a fool through lack of knowledge,
Vote wrong? If learning is no guide
Why ought one to have been in college?
O Son of Day, O Son of Night!
What are your preferences made of?
I know not which of you is right,
Nor which to be the more afraid of.
The world is old and the world is bad,
And creaks and grinds upon its axis;
And man's an ape and the gods are mad!
There's nothing sure, not even our taxes!
No mortal man can Truth restore,
Or say where she is to be sought for.
I know what uniform I wore
O, that I knew which side I fought for!

The Humorist

'What is that, mother?'
'The funny man, child.
His hands are black, but his heart is mild.'
'May I touch him, mother?'
''T were foolishly done:
He is slightly touched already, my son.'
'O, why does he wear such a ghastly grin?'
'That's the outward sign of a joke within.'
'Will he crack it, mother?'
'Not so, my saint;
'T is meant for the Saturday Liver complaint.'
'Does he suffer, mother?'
'God help him, yes!
A thousand and fifty kinds of distress.'
'What makes him sweat so?'
'The demons that lurk
In the fear of having to go to work.'
'Why doesn't he end, then, his life with a rope?'
'Abolition of Hell has deprived him of hope.'

The In-Coming Climate

Now o' nights the ocean breeze
Makes the patient flinch,
For that zephyr bears a sneeze
In every cubic inch.
Lo! the lively population
Chorusing in sternutation
A catarrhal acclamation!

The Key Note

I dreamed I was dreaming one morn as I lay
In a garden with flowers teeming.
On an island I lay in a mystical bay,
In the dream that I dreamed I was dreaming.
The ghost of a scent - had it followed me there
From the place where I truly was resting?
It filled like an anthem the aisles of the air,
The presence of roses attesting.
Yet I thought in the dream that I dreamed I dreamed
That the place was all barren of roses
That it only seemed; and the place, I deemed,
Was the Isle of Bewildered Noses.
Full many a seaman had testified

How all who sailed near were enchanted,
And landed to search (and in searching died)
For the roses the Sirens had planted.
For the Sirens were dead, and the billows boomed
In the stead of their singing forever;
But the roses bloomed on the graves of the doomed,
Though man had discovered them never.
I thought in my dream 'twas an idle tale,
A delusion that mariners cherished
That the fragrance loading the conscious gale
Was the ghost of a rose long perished.
I said, 'I will fly from this island of woes.'
And acting on that decision,
By that odor of rose I was led by the nose,
For 'twas truly, ah! truly, Elysian.
I ran, in my madness, to seek out the source
Of the redolent river directed
By some supernatural, sinister force
To a forest, dark, haunted, infected.
And still as I threaded ('twas all in the dream
That I dreamed I was dreaming) each turning
There were many a scream and a sudden gleam
Of eyes all uncannily burning!
The leaves were all wet with a horrible dew
That mirrored the red moon's crescent,
And all shapes were fringed with a ghostly blue,
Dim, wavering, phosphorescent.
But the fragrance divine, coming strong and free,
Led me on, though my blood was clotting,
Till - ah, joy! I could see, on the limbs of a tree,
Mine enemies hanging and rotting!

The King Of Bores

Abundant bores afflict this world, and some
Are bores of magnitude that come and no,
They're always coming, but they never go
Like funeral pageants, as they drone and hum
Their lurid nonsense like a muffled drum,
Or bagpipe's dread unnecessary flow.
But one superb tormentor I can show
Prince Fiddlefaddle, Duc de Feefawfum.
He the johndonkey is who, when I pen
Amorous verses in an idle mood
To nobody, or of her, reads them through
And, smirking, says he knows the lady; then
Calls me sly dog. I wish he understood
This tender sonnet's application too.

The Last Man

I dreamed that Gabriel took his horn
On Resurrection's fateful morn,
And lighting upon Laurel Hill
Blew long, blew loud, blew high and shrill.
The houses compassing the ground
Rattled their windows at the sound.
But no one rose. 'Alas!' said he,
'What lazy bones these mortals be!'
Again he plied the horn, again
Deflating both his lungs in vain;
Then stood astonished and chagrined
At raising nothing but the wind.
At last he caught the tranquil eye
Of an observer standing by
Last of mankind, not doomed to die.
To him thus Gabriel: 'Sir, I pray
This mystery you'll clear away.
Why do I sound my note in vain?
Why spring they not from out the plain?
Where's Luning, Blythe and Michael Reese,
Magee, who ran the Golden Fleece?
Where's Asa Fisk? Jim Phelan, who
Was thought to know a thing or two
Of land which rose but never sank?
Where's Con O'Conor of the Bank,
And all who consecrated lands
Of old by laying on of hands?
I ask of them because their worth
Was known in all they wished the earth.
Brisk boomers once, alert and wise,
Why don't they rise, why don't they rise?'
The man replied: 'Reburied long
With others of the shrouded throng
In San Mateo carted there
And dumped promiscuous, anywhere,
In holes and trenches - all misfits
Mixed up with one another's bits:
One's back-bone with another's shin,
A third one's skull with a fourth one's grin
Your eye was never, never fixed
Upon a company so mixed!
Go now among them there and blow:
'Twill be as good as any show
To see them, when they hear the tones,
Compiling one another's bones!
But here 'tis vain to sound and wait:
Naught rises here but real estate.
I own it all and shan't disgorge.
Don't know me? I am Henry George.'

The Legatee

In fair San Francisco a good man did dwell,
And he wrote out a will, for he didn't feel well.
Said he: 'It is proper, when making a gift,
To stimulate virtue by comforting thrift.'
So he left all his property, legal and straight,
To 'the cursedest rascal in all of the State.'
But the name he refused to insert, for, said he:
'Let each man consider himself legatee.'
In due course of time that philanthropist died,
And all San Francisco, and Oakland beside
Save only the lawyers came each with his claim,
The lawyers preferring to manage the same.
The cases were tried in Department Thirteen,
Judge Murphy presided, sedate and serene,
But couldn't quite specify, legal and straight,
The cursedest rascal in all of the State.
And so he remarked to them, little and big
To claimants: 'You skip!' and to lawyers: 'You dig!'
They tumbled, tumultuous, out of his court
And left him victorious, holding the fort.
'Twas then that he said: 'It is plain to my mind
This property's ownerless - how can I find
The cursedest rascal in all of the State?'
So he took it himself, which was legal and straight.

The Legend Of Immortal Truth

A bear, having spread him a notable feast,
Invited a famishing fox to the place.
'I've killed me,' quoth he, 'an edible beast
As ever distended the girdle of priest
With 'spread of religion,' or 'inward grace.'
To my den I conveyed her,
I bled her and flayed her,
I hung up her skin to dry;
Then laid her naked, to keep her cool,
On a slab of ice from the frozen pool;
And there we will eat her - you and I.'
The fox accepts, and away they walk,
Beguiling the time with courteous talk.
You'd ne'er have suspected, to see them smile,
The bear was thinking, the blessed while,
How, when his guest should be off his guard,
With feasting hard,
He'd give him a 'wipe' that would spoil his style.
You'd never have thought, to see them bow,

The fox was reflecting deeply how
He would best proceed, to circumvent
His host, and prig. The entire pig
Or other bird to the same intent.
When Strength and Cunning in love combine,
Be sure 't is to more than merely dine.
The while these biters ply the lip,
A mile ahead the muse shall skip:
The poet's purpose she best may serve
Inside the den - if she have the nerve.
Behold! laid out in dark recess,
A ghastly goat in stark undress,
Pallid and still on her gelid bed,
And indisputably very dead.
Her skin depends from a couple of pins
And here the most singular statement begins;
For all at once the butchered beast,
With easy grace for one deceased,
Upreared her head,
Looked round, and said,
Very distinctly for one so dead:
'The nights are sharp, and the sheets are thin:
I find it uncommonly cold herein!'
I answer not how this was wrought:
All miracles surpass my thought.
They're vexing, say you? and dementing?
Peace, peace! they're none of my inventing.
But lest too much of mystery
Embarrass this true history,
I'll not relate how that this goat
Stood up and stamped her feet, to inform'em
With what's the word? I mean, to warm'em;
Nor how she plucked her rough capote
From off the pegs where Bruin threw it,
And o'er her quaking body drew it;
Nor how each act could so befall:
I'll only swear she did them all;
Then lingered pensive in the grot,
As if she something had forgot,
Till a humble voice and a voice of pride
Were heard, in murmurs of love, outside.
Then, like a rocket set aflight,
She sprang, and streaked it for the light!
Ten million million years and a day
Have rolled, since these events, away;
But still the peasant at fall of night,
Belated therenear, is oft affright
By sounds of a phantom bear in flight;
A breaking of branches under the hill;
The noise of a going when all is still!
And hens asleep on the perch, they say,

Cackle sometimes in a startled way,
As if they were dreaming a dream that mocks
The lope and whiz of a fleeting fox!
Half we're taught, and teach to youth,
And praise by rote,
Is not, but merely stands for, truth.
So of my goat:
She's merely designed to represent
The truth - 'immortal' to this extent:
Dead she may be, and skinned frappe
Hid in a dreadful den away;
Prey to the Churches (any will do,
Except the Church of me and you.)
The simplest miracle, even then,
Will get her up and about again.

The Lord's Prayer On A Coin
Upon this quarter-eagle's leveled face,
The Lord's Prayer, legibly inscribed, I trace.
'Our Father which' the pronoun there is funny,
And shows the scribe to have addressed the money
'Which art in Heaven' an error this, no doubt:
The preposition should be stricken out.
Needless to quote; I only have designed
To praise the frankness of the pious mind
Which thought it natural and right to join,
With rare significancy, prayer and coin.

The Lost Colonel
"'Tis a woeful yarn,' said the sailor man bold
Who had sailed the northern lakes
'No woefuler one has ever been told
Exceptin' them called 'fakes.'"
'Go on, thou son of the wind and fog,
For I burn to know the worst!'
But his silent lip in a glass of grog
Was dreamily immersed.
Then he wiped it on his sleeve and said:
'It's never like that I drinks
But what of the gallant gent that's dead
I truly mournful thinks.
'He was a soldier chap - leastways
As 'Colonel' he was knew;
An' he hailed from some'rs where they raise
A grass that's heavenly blue.
'He sailed as a passenger aboard
The schooner 'Henery Jo.'

O wild the waves and galeses roared,
Like taggers in a show!
'But he sat at table that calm an' mild
As if he never had let
His sperit know that the waves was wild
An' everlastin' wet!
'Jest set with a bottle afore his nose,
As was labeled 'Total Eclipse'
(The bottle was) an' he frequent rose
A glass o' the same to his lips.
'An' he says to me (for the steward slick
Of the 'Henery Jo' was I):
'This sailor life's the very old Nick
On the lakes it's powerful dry!'
'I says: 'Aye, aye, sir, it beats the Dutch.
I hopes you'll outlast the trip.'
But if I'd been him - an' I said as much
I'd 'a' took a faster ship.
'His laughture, loud an' long an' free,
Rang out o'er the tempest's roar.
'You're an elegant reasoner,' says he,
'But it's powerful dry ashore!"
'O mariner man, why pause and don
A look of so deep concern?
Have another glass - go on, go on,
For to know the worst I burn.'
'One day he was leanin' over the rail,
When his footing some way slipped,
An' (this is the woefulest part o' my tale),
He was accidental unshipped!
'The empty boats was overboard hove,
As he swum in the 'Henery's wake';
But 'fore we had 'bouted ship he had drove
From sight on the ragin' lake!'
'And so the poor gentleman was drowned
And now I'm apprised of the worst.'
'What! him? 'Twas an hour afore he was found
In the yawl stone dead o' thirst!'

The Mackaiad

Mackay's hot wrath to Bonynge, direful spring
Of blows unnumbered, heavenly goddess, sing
That wrath which hurled to Hellman's office floor
Two heroes, mutually smeared with gore,
Whose hair in handfuls marked the dire debate,
And riven coat-tails testified their hate.
Sing, muse, what first their indignation fired,
What words augmented it, by whom inspired.
First, the great Bonynge comes upon the scene

And asks the favor of the British Queen.
Suppliant he stands and urges all his claim:
His wealth, his portly person and his name,
His habitation in the setting sun,
As child of nature; and his suit he won.
No more the Sovereign, wearied with his plea,
From slumber's chain her faculties can free.
Low and more low the royal eyelids creep,
She gives the assenting nod and falls asleep.
Straightway the Bonynges all invade the Court
And telegraph the news to every port.
Beneath the seas, red-hot, the tidings fly,
The cables crinkle and the fishes fry!
The world, awaking like a startled bat,
Exclaims: 'A Bonynge? What the devil's that?'
Mackay, meanwhile, to envy all attent,
Untaught to spare, unable to relent,
Walks in our town on needles and on pins,
And in a mean, revengeful spirit-grins!
Sing, muse, what next to break the peace occurred
What act uncivil, what unfriendly word?
The god of Bosh ascending from his pool,
Where since creation he has played the fool,
Clove the blue slush, as other gods the sky,
And, waiting but a moment's space to dry,
Touched Bonynge with his finger-tip. 'O son,'
He said, 'alike of nature and a gun,
Knowest not Mackay's insufferable sin?
Hast thou not heard that he doth stand and grin?
Arise! assert thy manhood, and attest
The uncommercial spirit in thy breast.
Avenge thine honor, for by Jove I swear
Thou shalt not else be my peculiar care!'
He spake, and ere his worshiper could kneel
Had dived into his slush pool, head and heel.
Full of the god and to revenges nerved,
And conscious of a will that never swerved,
Bonynge set sail: the world beyond the wave
As gladly took him as the other gave.
New York received him, but a shudder ran
Through all the western coast, which knew the man;
And science said that the seismic action
Was owing to an asteroid's impaction.
O goddess, sing what Bonynge next essayed.
Did he unscabbard the avenging blade,
The long spear brandish and porrect the shield,
Havoc the town and devastate the field?
His sacred thirst for blood did he allay
By halving the unfortunate Mackay?
Small were the profit and the joy to him
To hew a base born person, limb from limb.

Let vulgar souls to low revenge incline,
That of diviner spirits is divine.
Bonynge at noonday stood in public places
And (with regard to the Mackays) made faces!
Before those formidable frowns and scowls
The dogs fled, tail-tucked, with affrighted howls,
And horses, terrified, with flying feet
O'erthrew the apple-stands along the street,
Involving the metropolis in vast
Financial ruin! Man himself, aghast,
Retreated east and west and north and south
Before the menace of that twisted mouth,
Till Jove, in answer to their prayers, sent Night
To veil the dreadful visage from their sight!
Such were the causes of the horrid strife
The mother wrongs which nourished it to life.
O, for a quill from an archangel's wing!
O, for a voice that's adequate to sing
The splendor and the terror of the fray,
The scattered hair, the coat-tails all astray,
The parted collars and the gouts of gore
Reeking and smoking on the banker's floor,
The interlocking limbs, embraces dire,
Revolving bodies and deranged attire!
Vain, vain the trial: 'tis vouchsafed to none
To sing two millionaires rolled into one!
My hand and pen their offices refuse,
And hoarse and hoarser grows the weary muse.
Alone remains, to tell of the event,
Abandoned, lost and variously rent,
The Bonynge nethermost habiliment.

The Mad Philosopher

The flabby wine-skin of his brain
Yields to some pathologic strain,
And voids from its unstored abysm
The driblet of an aphorism.

Ambrose Bierce – A Short Biography

Ambrose Gwinnett Bierce had a diverse literary, military and journalistic career, during which his sardonic view of human nature ensured he was both frequently critical and frequently criticised. As a writer, his work included short stories, fables, editorials and his journalism, which was often controversial owing to his vehemence and acerbic style.

He was born on June 24th 1842 to Marcus Aurelius Bierce (1799-1876) and Laura Sherwood Bierce at Horse Cave Creek in Meigs Country, Ohio. Though his parents were poor they were literarily inclined and they introduced Bierce to this passion at an early age, instilling in him a deep appreciation of books, the written word and the elegance of language.

Bierce grew up in Koscuisko Country, Indiana, attending school at the county seat in Warsaw. He was the tenth of thirteen children, all of whom Marcus Aurelius gave names beginning with 'A', an indication of his love of poetry and alliteration. In order of birth they were Abigail, Amelia, Ann, Addison, Aurelius, Augustus, Almeda, Andrew, Albert, Ambrose, Arthur, Adelia and Aurelia. Poverty and religion were defining features of his childhood, and he would later describe his parents as "unwashed savages" and fanatically religious, showing him little affection but quick to punish him "with anything they could lay their hand on". He soon came to resent religion, and an introduction to literature is about the only lasting effect Marcus Aurelius had on Bierce.

Instead, Bierce began to respect his Uncle Lucius, whose "political and military distinction won the admiration of his nephew"; as an important figure within the American military and a graduate of Ohio University, he seemed far more worthy of admiration than his father. The family moved Westward when he was nine "in search of better land, and a more promising future", settling on 80 acres of farmland in Walnut Creek, Indiana.

Then, at the age of fifteen, Bierce left home to become a printer's devil, mixing ink and fetching type at The Northern Indian, a small Ohio newspaper run by a man named Reuben Williams. The duration of his time here is uncertain, though it is known that he quit the apprenticeship; apparently after being falsely accused of a theft. He returned to the family farm and spent time sending work to editors in the hopes of being published, though he was met with frequent rejection.

On the recommendation of his Uncle Lucius he was sent to the Kentucky Military Institute where, after a year's education, he was commissioned as an Officer in the Union Army. At the outset of the American Civil War in 1861, Bierce enlisted in the Union Army's 9th Indiana Infantry Regiment. His first major participation was during the Operations in Western Virginia campaign of 1861, and he was present at the 'first battle' at Philippi.

At the Battle of Rich Mountain on July 11th 1861 he executed the daring rescue of a gravely wounded comrade under heavy enemy fire, an act of bravery which received attention in the newspaper. Following this triumph he was commissioned First Lieutenant, serving as a topographical engineer on the staff of General William Babcock Hazen, undertaking the important work of making maps of likely battlefields.

In April 1862 Bierce fought at the Battle of Shiloh, an experience which, though terrifying, became the source of several of his short stories in later years, along with the memoir What I Saw of Shiloh. Two more years of valuable service followed until June 1864 when, while fighting at the Battle of Kennesaw Mountain, he sustained a serious head wound which required him to spend the summer on furlough, an unpaid yet honourable period of leave, in order to recover. He returned to active duty in September of that year, only to be discharged in January 1865 towards the close of the war.

However midway through 1866 he rejoined General Hazen on his expedition to inspect military outposts across the Great Plains, proceeding by horseback and wagon from Omaha, Nebraska, to San Francisco, California, at the end of the year.

While still in San Francisco, Bierce was presented with the rank of brevet major before tendering his resignation from the Army, choosing to remain in San Francisco and becoming involved with publishing and editing. On Christmas Day of 1871 Bierce married Mary Ellen, also known as Molly, with whom he had his first child, Day, the following year.

Later in 1872 he moved to England where he lived and wrote between the years 1872 and 1875, contributing work to Fun magazine. In 1874 his second son, Leigh, was born, and while in England he saw his first book, The Fiend's Delight, published by John Camden Hotton under the pseudonym 'Dod Grile'. It appeared in London in 1873, and was a collection of his articles. On the back of this success he was published twice more, first Nuggets and Dust Panned Out in California in 1873, and the next year Cobwebs from and Empty Skull, both collections of stories, fables, maxims, sketches, poetry, epigrams, quips and witticisms.

After this success and his continued regular contribution to Fun, he returned to San Francisco where he took up a more permanent residence and focused on his editorial career, working for a number of local papers including The San Francisco News Letter, The Argonaut, the Overland Monthly, The Californian and The Wasp. His crime writing was some of the finest of the medium and was reproduced in the Library of America anthology True Crime. His novella 'The Dance of Death', co-written with Thomas A. Harcourth for which he used the pseudonym William Herman was published in 1877, and then from 1879 to 1880 he travelled to the Dakota Territory, visiting Rockerville and Deadwood and experimenting with a managerial role at a New York mining company.

With the failure of that company he returned to San Francisco to continue his journalism, where in 1887 he began a column at the San Francisco Examiner named 'Prattle', which saw him become one of William Randolph Hearst's first regular columnists and editors at the paper. He eventually became one of the more influential and prominent of the journalists and writers of the West Coast. His association with Hearst Newspapers would continue until 1906.

Bierce's marriage was to fall apart when in 1888 he discovered compromising letters to his wife from a secret admirer. This led to their separation. The following year, 1889 his first son Day committed suicide following depression brought on by a romantic rejection.

In 1891, inspired by his time in the Union Army, Bierce wrote and published the collection of 26 short stories, Tales of Soldiers and Civilians which included his famous 'An Occurrence at Owl Creek Bridge'. Maintaining in the preface to the first edition that the book had been "denied existence by the chief publishing houses in the country", the eventual publication is accredited to his friend Mr E.L.G. Steele, a San Franciscan merchant against whose name the 1891 copyright is listed. The heavy irony of his depictions of battlefield heroism and valour perhaps reflects his own response to the differences between his act of human bravery, rescuing a comrade, and the 'brave sacrifices' of troop leaders whose stubborn and rash decisions often led to the deaths of many whose lives could have been spared by more prudent warmongering. A particular example of this is found in the actions of Lieutenant Brayle, of the story 'Incident at Resaca', in whose orders for a hundred men to charge gloriously into certain death Bierce presents valourous sacrifice, ideally rendered, but it is a portrayal which he then juxtaposes against the gruesomely realistic descriptions of their wounds and deaths. Moreover, alongside these informed accounts of battlefield brutality he acknowledges the frequent injuries sustained by women and children which were oft overlooked by official accounts and propaganda.

Three more publications followed, a book of poetry in 1892 entitled Black Beetles in Amber, followed by a novella, again co-written but this time with Adolphe De Castro named The Monk and the Hangman's Daughter, also published in 1892 and Can Such Things Be?, a collection of short stories which reached print in 1893. By this time the Union Pacific and Central Pacific railroad companies were receiving huge loans from the United States Government towards their endeavours to build the First Transcontinental Railroad, and Collis P. Huntingdon sought to introduce a bill which quietly excused the companies from repaying the money, essentially converting the loan into a handout of $130 million dollars. The plot's essence was secrecy, for its perpetrators hoped to get the bill through Congress without any public notice and subsequent hearing, so in 1896 Hearst dispatched Bierce to Washington, D.C to scupper their plans. Confronted by Huntingdon on the steps of the Capitol and angrily invited to name his price, Bierce answered "my price is $130 million dollars. If, when you are ready to pay, I happen to be out of town, you may hand it over to my friend, the Treasurer of the United States". This answer became famous and was recorded in newspapers nationwide, and his coverage of and diatribes on the issue encouraged such public outrage that the bill was challenged and defeated. Following this huge success, Bierce returned to California in November.

He now began his first foray into a career as a fabulist, publishing Fantastic Fables in 1899 and anticipating the rise of ironic grotesquerie which was seen in the 20th century. The following year, owing to his penchant for stirring up the public through his biting satire and social criticism, he induced a hostile reaction to a poem he had written in 1900 about the assassination of Governor Goebel and following the assassination of President William McKinley which had been deliberately misconstrued by Hearst's opponents, turning it into something of a cause célèbre. The poem was meant to express the national sense of fear and dismay at Goebel's death, but the lines

> The bullet that pierced Goebel's breast
> Can not be found in all the West;
> Good reason, it is speeding here
> To stretch McKinley on his bier

(written innoculously in 1900) seemed to foreshadow the subsequent shooting on McKinley in 1901. This saw Hearst accused of having called for McKinley's assassination by his rivals and then by Elihu Root, then Secretary of State, though despite the national uproar which ended Hearst's ambitions for presidency, Bierce was never revealed as the author of the poem; nor, indeed, did Hearst ever fire him from the paper.

In 1901, his second son Leigh died of pneumonia relating to his alcoholism.

His enduring career at the paper was accompanied by several more publications, the next of which was Shapes of Clay in 1903, a book of poetry and the first publication of one of his most famous works, The Devil's Dictionary, which began life as an occasional newspaper item of satirical definitions of English words and then, in 1906, was published as a collection in book form under the name The Cynic's Word Book. In 1909 The Cynic's Word Book was reprinted under its current name, which Bierce himself preferred, as the entirety of the seventh volume of his Collected Works which brought together the majority of his short stories and poems. The same year he wrote Write it Right, a non-fiction work of literary criticism and commentary, which appeared alongside The Shadow on the Dial, and other essays. However, despite this professional success he finally divorced his wife in 1904, and she died the following year.

At the age of 71, in 1913 Bierce departed from Washington, D.C., for a tour of the battlefields upon which he had fought during the civil war. He had passed through Louisiana and Texas by December and was crossing into by way of El Paso into Mexico which was itself in the throes of revolution. He joined Pancho Villa's army as an observer in Ciudad Juárez during which time he witnessed the battle of Tierra Blanca. It is known that he accompanied Villa's army as far as the city of Chihuahua where he wrote his last known communication in the form of a letter to Blanche Partington, one of his close friends, dated 26th December 1913. He closed the letter with the words "as to me, I leave here tomorrow for an unknown destination" and then vanished without trace in what would become one of the most famous unexplained disappearances in American history. Various suggestions have been posited, including that belonging to the oral tradition of Sierra Mojada, Coahuila, which holds that Bierce was executed by firing squad in the town cemetery there. All that is known is that, by this time, he was suffering considerably from the asthma which had dogged him throughout his life and was compounded by his war injuries.

In 1920, three of his stories A Horseman in the Sky, A Watcher by the Dead and The Man and the Snake were published posthumously, and further poetry was published in 1980 under the title A Vision of Doom: Poems by Ambrose Pierce. As a writer, he often found himself splitting opinion and continues to do so in death, his writing variously described as cheap and vulgar, and conversely the best writing on war and that of a flawless American genius. Regardless of how differently his critics speak of him, his legacy is one of concise, acerbic and cruelly satirical social commentary, an authorial style of economy, fruitful observation and as a judicious wordsmith.

www.ingramcontent.com/pod-product-compliance
Lightning Source LLC
Chambersburg PA
CBHW071722040426
42446CB00011B/2173